FOR PEACE WITHIN

*

SERMONS FOR THE LENTEN
and
EASTER SEASON

082368

*

By

O. A. Geiseman, S.T.D.

Pastor of Grace Lutheran Church, River Forest, Illinois

Ernst Kaufmann, Inc.

NEW YORK . CHICAGO

DEDICATION

To all of my co-workers on the staff of Grace Church whose whole-hearted loyalty, helpful cooperation, and earnest devotion to Christ and duty contribute to the joys of my ministry, this volume is gratefully dedicated.

PREFACE

Many persons of our day seem to think that psychology is a substitute for religion. Psychology, as every pastor, educator, and student of human nature knows, is making an important contribution in its field. While it may serve well to assist in the analysis of behavior and personality problems, it is not qualified to provide men with true peace of heart. Merely to verbalize one's difficulties and worries or to ferret out, at least in part, their origins does not yet provide a lasting and satisfying answer. Peace of heart will come only to him who is assured of peace with his God.

The messages contained in this volume were presented for the purpose of leading men to Christ, their Redeemer, without whom "no man cometh to the Father" or finds that "peace which surpasseth all understanding." Two series of Lenten addresses plus additional messages for Palm Sunday, Maundy Thursday, Good Friday, and Easter are herewith presented. It is my hope and prayer that they may serve to bring peace of heart to all who read them and that they will point the way, at least in a modest measure, toward a helpful application of the Christian faith to some of the practical problems of life in a modern world.

THE AUTHOR.

Grace Lutheran Church
River Forest, Illinois
July 8, A.D., 1947

CONTENTS

First Series

Second Series

The Christ Of Our Salvation

HOW JESUS MET HIS TASK

✦   ✦   ✦

"When Jesus had spoken these words, He went forth with His disciples over the brook Cedron, where was a garden, into the which He entered, and His disciples. And Judas also, which betrayed Him, knew the place; for Jesus ofttimes resorted thither with His disciples." —John 18: 1-2.

✦   ✦   ✦

MAY it please the Spirit of God to be with us in this Lenten service and throughout the Lenten season so that our understanding of spiritual truths may be deepened, our spiritual life quickened, and our appreciation of Christ's redeeming love greatly increased for the Saviour's sake. Amen.

A TIME FOR SPIRITUAL GROWTH

Christians around the world have with this day entered upon a new holy season. The season of Lent is an invitation to every follower of Christ to engage in a very careful self-examination and to seek a fuller knowledge and appreciation of Christ's love and mercy. All who profess to be children of God should, of course, at all times be interested in the cultivation of their spiritual lives. Yet God's children have always found it expedient and profitable to set aside certain seasons for a special and more intensive application of their hearts and souls to the great spiritual and eternal truths. It was so in the church of the Old Covenant. It has been so in the church of the New Covenant. The season of Lent is one of these particular seasons.

Most of us have lived through a fair number of such seasons. It is doubtful whether we have always availed ourselves of the opportunity for spiritual growth which such seasons afford. Will you not in your own heart now address a quiet prayer to God that He will not let you go through this Lenten season without having come closer to Him, without having become a nobler son, a lovelier daughter of His. It shall be our aim in these services to try to help you in your thought, to guide you in your meditation on the suffering and death of Jesus and on the meaning of this great act of sacrificial love for you. But all guidance will be of little avail unless you whole-heartedly, earnestly, devotedly enter upon it, accept it and use it to the fullest advantage of your own soul.

This evening I would like to speak to you on a subject suggested by the beginning of the Passion Story. Our theme shall be, "How Jesus Met His Task."

We read in the Gospel according to St. John, the opening verses of chapter 18, "When Jesus had spoken these words He went forth with His disciples over the brook Kedron where was a Garden into the which He entered, and His disciples. And Judas also which betrayed Him knew the place for Jesus ofttimes resorted thither with His disciples."

JESUS HAD A TASK

Jesus had a task. It was a task which God had resolved upon in eternity. He spoke to man about it for the first time in Paradise. The prophets made it the very heart of their preaching. The heavenly messenger expressed it beautifully and simply when on the first Christmas Eve he said to the shepherds, "Unto you is born this day in the city of David a Savior, which is Christ the Lord." John the Baptist spoke about the Savior's task when at the beginning of His public ministry he pointed to Him and said, "Behold the Lamb of God which taketh away the sins of the world." Jesus spoke about His task, too. He said, "The Son of Man is come to seek and to save that which is lost."

This was an unusual task. No one in the world's history before that time or since that time ever was called upon to do what Jesus did. It was purely a task of love. There was not in it the slightest element of selfishness. It was all done for others not for Himself. Jesus went to the task of correcting the situation which had arisen between God and man. Jesus came to bring harmony between the creature and the Creator. Jesus came to remove the wall of sin which had grown up between the Father and His children. It was a glorious task, the task of the Redeemer of all mankind.

WE HAVE A TASK

Even as Jesus had His task, so have we our tasks. Probably we can group all we have to do in this world under three points. *Our first task is to get right with God.* You are not going to do anything right in this world unless you first get right with God. You are never going to know peace and happiness in your soul unless you first enter into harmony with Him who made you. So your first task in life is to accept Jesus as your Redeemer, to say in all the humility of your soul, "This is my Lord who has redeemed me, a lost and condemned creature."

When through faith in Christ you become a child of God then *it is your task to live as a child of God.* This means that you must overcome yourself. This is a great assignment. So many of us, I fear, have no conception either of its importance or of its difficulty. It is not so very long ago when one noon while lunching with a group of people I heard a man, a reasonably successful businessman, say, "I have no regrets in my life. I do not feel that I ever made any mistakes." I do not know how many such people there are who would in that same bland, bold way assert that they had nothing to regret, but I am sure that all of us are still not aware how great and hard a problem we really have in trying to overcome our own hearts. This calls for a great deal of introspection and self-analysis. You must practice looking on the inside. You must cultivate the ability to sit at the side of the road, as it were, and watch yourself go down the highway of life. You must study what goes on in your heart and in your mind, and then compare very carefully what you find with the things which God asks of you. Then you will learn what a job you have on your hands, what a real assignment God has given you when He asks you to crucify the flesh with all of its lusts and evil desires. But that is your task.

As a child of God and as a member of human society you also have the task of giving yourself to some wholesome and worthwhile work in life by which you can honestly and honorably earn your livelihood and do something that is good for your fellowmen. Many who are of the world do not understand it. They have no idea that they should earn their living in an honest and honorable way. The only thing they are concerned about is to get a living, whether by fair or foul means is of no particular concern to them. Whether by getting something for themselves they are disturbing the lives of others or destroying their morals or characters and undermining all of society leaves them quite cold and unaffected. Certainly, it ought not be so with us if we profess to be Christians.

Then you have the third task of exerting an influence for good in human society. This again falls into two divisions. On the one hand *you are to exercise a restraining influence in life*. You are to be like a dam that holds back the flood of sin. You are to be a salt in a world that is rotten with sin and that is in a constant process of moral decay and degeneration. You are to hold back this process so that human society can exist, for men abandoned to sin destroy themselves and all that is about them. So you see, you have a task. Jesus had a task, but He saw to it that you and I have a task and one that really calls for strenuous living. Here is a challenge. You dare not go the easy way. You dare not go with the mob. You should stand out as a child of God, as a follower of Jesus against everything that is wrong and sinful in this world.

But you are not only to restrain the evil influences in society, *you are also to make an impact on society and to recreate it so that the rottenness and the immorality of it is overcome and wholesome moral and spiritual living takes its place.* We are not in this community merely for our own good. This church does not stand just to house us when we have the impulse to worship God. This church stands here as a testimony to the whole community concerning certain divine truths of salvation. You as a member of the church and as a disciple of Jesus Christ have the responsibility to all that are about you and to all the world to bring to them the message of Christ. That is your task. You are to stem the tide of sin and to build the kingdom of God, win souls for Jesus, bring nobility into the lives of men, beautify homes and families, put the halo of glory about men as you sow the seed of the Gospel into individual hearts.

JESUS WENT TO HIS TASK

Jesus had a task, and we can see from the words of our text that *He went to His task*. He met it. He did not shirk it. No, He went with His eyes wide open, thoroughly conscious from step to step as to what it would cost, what it would take, how He would suffer, how it would end. At no time was there any illusion about the meaning of it all. With a quiet determination in His heart, Jesus went forth to meet His task.

GOOD NEWS

That is wonderfully good news for you and for me. It means that our blessed Lord, in complete obedience to the will of the Father, did what needed to be done to work out the salvation of our souls. Had Jesus not met His task I would have no message for you. I do not know where we would be, but I am sure we would not be here. And if we were here, no one could stand in this pulpit and say anything to us that could bring us peace and cheer. It is only because Jesus met His task, because He fulfilled God's will on our behalf and endured for us the things which we had merited, that we now, as poor sinners, can come to God in the full knowledge that we are washed clean of all of our iniquities by His holy and precious blood. If you can go to sleep tonight with the knowledge that the angels of God are hovering over you and that the omnipotent Lord who is behind the sun, the moon, and the stars, is looking down upon you with favor and with fatherly kindness and goodness in His heart, then all this is possible only because Jesus met His task. Cling to that and make the most of it. Draw out of it every drop of comfort it is designed to yield to you, for here is the real source of strength, of cheer in every circumstance and experience of life.

DETERMINATION

But as Jesus met His task, so you and I should meet our task. Jesus did it with determination. There was no wavering. He did not approach it carelessly, indifferently. No. With His whole heart and mind set to it, He went into the task. He did it as God wanted it done. But how are you doing your task? How are you approaching the whole matter of your own religious life? Just what are you giving to it, how much thought, how much attention? How much does it engross your heart and the interests and the energies of your life? Think of this one thing, harmony with God through faith in Jesus Christ. Just what are you doing about it? How are you meeting your task? You think about it. There is little need in my passing judgment on you. It is something between you and your God. But I can say to you, inasmuch as you are a human being, and inasmuch as there is sin in your heart, this is something to think about.

I don't think you will count it unfair if I say that we are all inclined to take our religion quite superficially and formally. We think about the love of Jesus, the awfulness of sin, as though they were the most commonplace things in life. We thrill more to some sport event, the winning of a ball game or a hockey game or some such thing as that, than we do to the proclamation of the Gospel of Jesus Christ. We get all excited about some things that happen in the world of politics or in the world of business, but we remain quite cold and unmoved about the story of the Christ. We really agonize about success in business, at our job, or when we fear that we are going to lose money, or that we are getting ill, or some such thing as that, but how much do we agonize about our souls? How concerned are you that there should be real peace and that there should be a loving relationship between God and yourself? How much of a conscious effort are you making every day of your life to overcome yourself, to be more like Christ tomorrow than you were today and the day after tomorrow than you will be tomorrow? Just how much of your time does that occupy? How much thought do you give

it?   How concerned are you about it in your soul?
Jesus went to His task. Are you going to your task?

SOCIAL RESPONSIBILITIES

And what are you doing about your responsibilities
over against society? God knows the world is in a bad
way. Yesterday a private citizen, who nevertheless has
consequence as an international voice warned against
certain dangers which exist in the relationship of the
great nations which only recently were fighting shoulder
to shoulder. The only answer he could give to it all was
to build up the military, to keep ourselves strong so that
no nation would dare defy us. Let us assume that that
is good advice. I don't know whether it is or whether
it is not from a purely international, governmental point
of view. But let us assume that it is good advice. How
good is it? What does it do? It only increases the
terror that is in human hearts and it does absolutely
nothing to make one single human being better than he
was before. It may only cause people to become more
aggressive and more determined to assert their power,
their might over their fellowmen. My friends, if that
is the kind of a condition the world is in, and very probably it is, then that means that you and I as the messengers of Jesus, as the light bearers, as the people who
march under the banner of the cross, have a real task
to do in this world of ours, and there is no time to be
lost. We are not merely to see how others are trumpet-
ing and then blow into the same trumpets with them.
We are not to accept the world's solutions. We have a
special assignment, because we profess to believe in
Jesus Christ. And if we believe in Him then we are to
devote ourselves to this job of giving them the Gospel,
of pleading with them, of showing them by our lives
what it means to be a Christian so that they will be

attracted to the fold of the Lord and join us in glorifying God. That is what our Lord said. That is our task. Jesus went to His task. Are you going to your task? Or are you so busy doing what the world does, trying to compete with the world on its own terms, that you cannot think of the fact that you are a Christian? Do you say that you have no time to be bothered about saving souls and about trying to tell those with whom you work, with whom you do business, that you are a Christian, that you have found something that really answers the needs of human hearts, that transforms life and puts hope into the human breast? Think about it. This is the time to think about it. This is Lent. Jesus went to His task and it was a tremendous one. God has paid you a wonderful compliment. He has given you a position of honor and dignity and responsibility such as nobody else in this world has. It is the distinctive responsibility of the Christian. What are you doing about your task?

PREPARATION FOR TASK

When Jesus went to His task He was determined, but He also knew that it was a difficult task and that He needed to be prepared for it, so He did not go into it carelessly feeling that He had everything it required. No, we are told He went to a Garden. We are told that He went to that Garden so often that even His enemies knew that He went there. And we know that He had a special reason for going to that Garden. He went, not only to sit around and listen to the song of the birds, no, He went to that Garden *to commune with the Father in prayer*. He called down the strength, the help and the blessing of God upon the thing which He was going to do. And this was not the only time He prayed.

I shall not take time to enumerate the instances of prayer on the part of Jesus referred to in the Gospels, but I want to assure you that even as Jesus relied upon prayer so *you and I will either rely upon prayer or fail.* Here is a fountain, a freely flowing fountain, into which we can dip and from which we can take at will all of God's help. He has put everything at our disposal, His love, His power, His wisdom, everything, and we need but lift our hearts and hands to Him and beg of Him and He will give. That is how Jesus prepared for His task. How are you preparing for yours?

We are such boastful creatures. It is so pitiful to hear us talk. We act as though we had the capacity to handle the situation by ourselves, and yet we are so impotent. We are so simple in our conception of what the forces of evil really represent. Jesus knew what it meant to meet hell and all the forces of evil. All the great sons and daughters of God through the ages have known what it meant. Martin Luther knew what it meant. He said, "With might of ours naught can be done." He prayed and all of God's sons and daughters have prayed. That is what we must do. If you want your individual life to be what God wants it to be, you must pray. If you want your family life to be as God would like it to be, you must pray. If you want the work of the church to be what by the mercies of God it can and should be, well, then, you must pray. You must pray for the blessings of God upon the work which is being done by our teachers and Sunday School teachers with the young. You must pray for the young assistant who goes as the ambassador of our church into home after home in our community, and is sometimes perhaps the first official representative of our church to greet people. Imagine the responsibility of that. And you must pray for me so that God will allow me so to teach and so to preach that there will be in it life, power, and meaning, so that the Spirit of God can use it in the hearts of men and achieve something.—My preaching is not to be merely another address which allows people to walk out untouched as though you had poured water over a duck's back. We must pray.

But if you will pray, if you will pray for yourself and your place in life, and if you will pray for the successful completion of God's purposes and God's plans for the good of mankind, oh, who will begin to say what we may be able to achieve for God and for our fellowmen?

Jesus achieved and because He did there are countless souls in glory surrounding the throne of the Lamb and joined with the heavenly chorus singing the praises of Him who made them and who redeemed them. See your task. Go to your task. Invite the help and the blessings of God for the achievement of your task. Then you cannot fail.

HOW JESUS MET HIS FOES

✦   ✦   ✦

"Judas then, having received a band of men and officers from the
chief priests and pharisees, cometh thither with lanterns and torches and
weapons. Jesus, therefore, knowing all things that should come upon
Him, went forth, and said unto them, 'Whom seek ye?' They answered
Him, 'Jesus of Nazareth.' Jesus saith unto them, 'I am He.' And
Judas also, which betrayed Him, stood with them. As soon then as He
had said unto them, 'I am He,' they went backward, and fell to the
ground. Then asked He them again, 'Whom seek ye?' And they said,
'Jesus of Nazareth.' Jesus answered, 'I have told you that I am He:
if therefore ye seek Me, let these go their way:' That the saying might
be fullfilled, which He spake, 'Of them which thou gavest Me have I
lost none. Then Simon Peter having a sword drew it, and smote the
high priest's servant, and cut off his right ear. The servant's name was
Malchus. Then said Jesus unto Peter, 'Put up thy sword into the
sheath: the cup which My Father had given Me, shall I not drink it?'
Then the band and the captain and officers of the Jews took Jesus, and
bound Him, And let Him away to Annas first; for he was father-in-law
to Caiaphas, which was the high priest that same year." John 18: 3-13.

✦   ✦   ✦

JESUS HAD ENEMIES

WE observe from the words of this text that
Jesus had enemies. It is difficult to understand
why He should have had enemies. Certainly if
anyone ever was good it was He. His words were true
and His life was pure and holy. If He dealt with men
it was only to be kind to them and to do them good. At
no time had anyone rightfully accused Him of any
wrong. He had befriended people of all walks of life.
He had passed no one by in a cold and heartless way.
Yet all of this did not suffice to protect Him against be-
coming the victim of foes.

When we observe who these foes were it again
strikes us rather queerly to know that they were people
in the church. Our text does not say that the harlots,

22

the publicans, the drunkards and people of such a class hated Him. No, it tells us that Judas and the Scribes and the Pharisees and such military servants as were assigned to them went out to take Jesus captive. We can understand why the Scribes and Pharisees could be so bitter against Jesus. Black never looks so black as it does when we put it against a white background. So was it with the sins of these people. Their hypocrisy, their religious formalism, which was utterly meaningless and blasphemous in character, stood out in bold relief when put against the background of the sincerity, the purity, the holiness and humility of Jesus, the Son of God Himself.

Even as Jesus had His enemies in that distant day so does He still have them. Some of His most effective foes are still within the organized church, within the number of those who profess to be children of God. No scoffer, no philosopher of this world who has promoted unbelief and agnosticism has done quite so much harm to the cause of Jesus as have those people who have stood in allegedly Christian pulpits and taught men to disbelieve the great truths of salvation. They are the people who have estranged the hearts of many from Christ and who have caused incredible numbers to disbelieve such great truths as the deity of Jesus, the inspiration of the Sacred Scriptures, the atoning sacrifice of our Lord on Calvary's Cross.

But it is not only the ministers in the church who disbelieve these truths who have become the enemies of Christ. Often also it is the people who sit in the pews of the churches and who use the church and religion merely as a mask. If you profess to be a Christian, you had better live like a Christian, because only so can you be a friend of Jesus. If you profess to be a Christian and then live like a worldling you are not a friend of

Jesus, you are His enemy. You are the kind of a person who causes people to blaspheme the holy name of God. Our Lord once said to the Children of Israel, "You make your boast in the law and then by transgressing the Law you cause the gentiles to blaspheme God." The Hebrew people were so proud of the fact that God had given them the Law by special revelation through Moses. They were so proud of the fact that He had given to them the Messianic promises through the mouths of His prophets, and they were not slow boasting about this in their contacts with gentile peoples. But when these gentiles observed how these people lived and how their life contradicted their boasting, it made them ridicule religion all the more. So the most effective and the most powerful enemies our Lord can have are the kind of people who either stand in a pulpit and deny the truths of Christianity or the kind of people who sit in the pews and by their lives contradict and deny everything they profess with their mouths. When we talk about the enemies of Jesus each one of us will do well to look into his own heart. You had better take a moment out to look into your own heart and see just who you are. Are you one of His friends or are you one of His enemies? Are you the kind of a person who is attracting people to Jesus and to the beauty of the Christian religion or are you the kind of a person who by the contradictions which exist between his professions and his living causes individuals to laugh at Christianity and to treat it with scorn and mockery as something for hypocrites and dishonest individuals?

WE, TOO, HAVE ENEMIES

If Jesus had enemies, as you can see He did have, you and I must not suppose that we are going to go through life without having them. When I speak about your enemies I imagine certain kinds of people will at once come to your mind. Perhaps you will think of individuals who are jealous and envious of you, perhaps because of your happiness, because of the lovely home in which you live, because of the success which you are having in your job or in your business. Perhaps you are thinking of someone in the relationship who does not like you and who goes out of his way to make life bitter for you. Well, they are enemies of course, but, my friends, they are not the particular enemies I have in mind when I want to urge upon you this evening the fact that you do have enemies. I am thinking especially of the enemies who are determined to destroy your soul. Your arch enemy is Satan who has a great host of allies. He works through many channels, through many different kinds of agencies. He is not particular by what means he brings about your destruction. He is only concerned about destroying you, whatever the means may be. The kind of a world in which you live lends itself well to the devil's purposes and he will use many of the things which you encounter in your everyday living in his endeavor to tear you away from the hands of divine mercy and to get you into his clutches so that he can throttle you, choke all spiritual life out of you, and rob you of your last hope. If you went with me on pastoral errands and encountered all of the things along life's way which I encounter, then you would know whereof I am speaking. I can assure you Satan has lost none of his subtleness. He appeared to Eve in the form of a serpent. He is just as subtle today.

When we read a story such as this it should make very clear to us that we have a Friend and we have a foe. There are always two forces struggling for your soul. One of these is God. He is consistently seeking to save your soul. God wants to take you up into His protecting hand. He wants to shield and shelter you in His fatherly em-

brace. He wants to carry you safely through all of life's
storms, through all of the pitfalls and bring you safely to
yonder goal. That is what divine love wants to do for you.
The Devil, the meanwhile, is trying to destroy your soul.
Make up your mind, one of these two forces will get you.
Either it will be God who will carry you into a life of
eternal blessedness or it will be the devil who will
destroy you.

You have enemies. The way in which the enemy
comes to you may be different from the way in which
he comes to me. His manner of coming to me may be
a little more subtle than his manner of coming to you.
I don't live right out in the stream of life as it were.
My life is a little more protected. But that doesn't mean
that the devil is not as much after me as he is after you.
Perhaps Christian ministers are his pet target, for when
he can get one of them then he really has done damage
to the kingdom. It will either be God or it will be the
devil who gets us, one or the other, and you and I had
better be awake to the fact. Don't act, therefore, as
though there were no dangers for your soul. It is really
alarming to see how unsophisticated we are in this respect. Every once in a while I encounter people who live
right out in the busy stream of life and who do not seem
to be aware of the danger in which they are. They behave as though they could play along with the world,
think like the world, live like the world and still be children of God. No, it cannot be. You are either a Christian and live like a Christian or you are an enemy of
Christ and the enemy of your soul is succeeding in
destroying you.

This is so terribly urgent for a congregation such as
ours because many of you are in greater danger than
others who occupy a more modest position in life. The
more successful you are, the more money you get, the

higher you rise, the more you learn, the more you think, the more will you become the target of Satan. It is not at all surprising that the devil concentrated all his forces on Jesus. He was the key person. If he could have destroyed Jesus the victory would have been complete. Then everybody would have been destroyed. So if you are wise, and if you are ready to let the Spirit of God open your eyes, then you will not go through life feeling altogether secure and sufficient unto yourself, but you will keep your eyes open and watch.

JESUS MET HIS FOES

Jesus went out to meet the foe. He knew what was going to happen when the enemy came. So He went forth and said, "Whom seek ye?" They answered, "Jesus of Nazareth." He said, "I am He." He did not want to disturb His disciples. He wanted all of the attack to be concentrated on Himself because He was the One who had come to suffer and die for the redemption of mankind and this was the hour of darkness. This, now, was the real thing. Now everything was heading up toward the eventual climax.

JESUS DID NOT USE FORCE

When Jesus met the enemy, Peter had his own ideas as to how the situation ought be handled. He hurriedly reached for his sword and began to strike to the right and to the left. He chopped off the ear of one of the high priest's servants. Peter was a vigorous character. He was very impulsive and it didn't take him very long to make up his mind. He acted and he spoke very quickly. He did also in this case. But Jesus did not believe in Peter's methods. He said to Peter, "Put up thy sword into the sheathe."

The method which Peter wanted to employ to protect Jesus and promote Christ's cause has often been attempted throughout the existence of the church. There has hardly been a time in the history of the Christian religion when there was not somebody who thought that the way to build the church of God was by using the sword. This was the basic principle underlying the Inquisition. The inquisitors believed that they were the most loyal sons of God. They really thought that they were promoting the glory of Jesus and that they were building the kingdom of the Lord when they burned people at the stake or put them on the rack, and when under threat of death they made them confess what they thought was the truth of God.

There are potential inquisitors at all times. I imagine if we were to call a convention of all of us here tonight and discuss how we ought handle certain present-day social problems we would find that one or another would express the thought that we ought to pass some laws, that we ought to make people behave, that we ought compel them by the sword, by threat of imprisonment, fine, or something to become children of God. This idea of passing laws and of getting the government behind the church was really basically the idea which Peter had, but Jesus wanted to have nothing to do with such a method. When we observe the ministry of Christ we discover that He never tried to overcome an enemy of His by force. Jesus knew that you cannot conquer the human heart and the human spirit by force.

Even though Jesus did not resort to force, however, He still was completely master of the situation. It was not the enemies who overwhelmed Him, it was He who overwhelmed the enemies. He went forth and said, "Whom seek ye?" They said, "Jesus of Nazareth." He said, "I am He." When He said this they all fell to the ground as though they were paralyzed with fear. No

wonder they were paralyzed. When a sinner stands in
the presence of the Holy One, how else can He be?
Imagine someone wanting to lay the hands of violence
on the person of God's only-begotten Son! Just think
how men, conscious of their sins, would shrink from such
a thing. They would realize what a dastardly thing
it was to try to take captive the Holy One of God. When
Jesus said, "I am He," that was too much for them. But
still Jesus understood the situation and so He drank the
cup of suffering and allowed Himself to be bound.

JESUS THE MASTER

There are a number of truths in this which have
tremendous practical significance for us. Let me remind
you that this scene in the Passion of our Lord reveals
to us in its own clear way the complete mastery of Jesus.
Sometimes we wonder just what is going to happen to
the church. What will happen to the church if materialism continues to grow and if the idea of atheistic communism continues to spread? What will happen to the
church if some of the educators and scientists of our
land and all those who ape them are going to be enemies
of Christ? What will happen to the church if the people
in the church become a part of the world so that you can
not distinguish the believer from the unbeliever by his
behavior? Really, one becomes worried just looking at
it from a human point of view. But you and I will never
have to worry as to what will become of the kingdom of
God. The kingdom of God will go on. The only thing
about which you and I must be worried is the part we
are going to play in its upbuilding and extension. If
you and I don't build the kingdom of God that does not
mean that it is not going to be built. No, Jesus will take
the torch of saving truth from our hands and pass it
along to someone else who will hold it aloft. If Grace
Church falls away from God, if the members of Grace

Church are not ready to build the kingdom of Christ, that does not mean that our Lord's cause is going to be lost, not at all. It only means that you and I will have no part in it. The cause will go on because Jesus is the Master. He absolutely controls even the lives, the powers, and the hearts of His enemies. They can do no more than at any moment He will permit them to do.

OUR COMFORT

The very fact, however, that Jesus was the Master of this situation and still drank the cup of sorrow is what brings comfort to our hearts. If these people had overwhelmed Jesus, well then they would have been the masters and He would have been the unwilling victim on the cross. But that was not how it was. We read, "Jesus, therefore, knowing all things that should come upon Him, went forth." Although with a word He could make His enemies helpless, yet He allowed them to bind His hands and lead Him away a captive.

Here was the willing servant of God going forth to carry out God's plan for the redemption of mankind, and, my friends, this must be your comfort now. When I say to you, as I did say, that you hurt Jesus and act like His enemy when you do not live in harmony with your Christian professions, then you are struck in your conscience because you know full well that there have been times when you have done just that. This does not mean, however, that Jesus does not want anything more to do with you. No, He still loves you. His love and mercy are still reaching out for you. He doesn't want to abandon you to the forces of evil. He doesn't want you to be torn headlong into the whirlpool of certain destruction. He wants to get hold of you, lift you out, rescue and save you. It was for this He willingly suffered. When Jesus let Himself be bound and led away, when He let Himself be nailed to the cross, He did it, not because the enemy had overwhelmed Him, but because He was ready to suffer what you should have suffered on account of your sins. So in this very willingness of Jesus lies a sweet note of comfort for your heart. No matter what your behavior may have been in the past, get everything right with God now. That was why Jesus gave Himself into captivity so that you could be free from the bonds of sin. That is why He shed His holy and precious blood, so you could be washed clean from all the dark black stains of sin that are upon your soul and conscience. So make your peace with God now and let this be a reassuring truth to you. All has been done for you by Jesus. Accept Him. Trust in Him. Believe in Him, and don't go out of this house of God until you have resolved that with Christ in your heart your conscience shall be free and you are going to be a happy child of God. No longer are you going to allow fears and an evil conscience to torture and torment you. No, you are going to be a blessed son or daughter of God.

WE CAN BE MASTERS

This beautiful record should teach us that even as Jesus had the mastery over His enemies, so can we through Christ gain mastery over evil. The enemies who attack us are the same ones who attacked Jesus. The force behind them is always the same. We have one enemy who goes about as a roaring lion seeking whom he may devour. But if you will take Jesus Christ, if you will let Him be your ally, if you will let Him be the Champion of your cause, then there is no enemy whom you cannot defeat.

It is not hard to get into the clutches of sin. It all comes very imperceptibly. You notice Judas again plays a prominent part in this story. Poor Judas! Step by step without realizing it, he came to the point where he sold his Lord for thirty pieces of silver. First a disciple of Jesus, then a traitor! Gradually, imperceptibly he went from one extreme to the other. That is how the devil works. That is how he will try to work with you. He will scarcely try to take you from the church all at once. He won't try to take you as one who earnestly believes today and change you into an infidel tomorrow. Not at all. He will take you gradually so that before you realize what has happened to you, you have lost your interest in God and His Church. You may still associate with members of the church, but you are actually no longer one of God's children. You may not have noticed what was happening. You may not believe that this could happen to you, but it can.

While it can happen to you, it need not happen to you. The fact that you are not strong enough to resist, the fact that you are not smart enough to outwit Satan, does not mean that he may not be out-smarted and defeated. He can and should be defeated with the help of Jesus Christ. The Savior is here ready to send His Holy Spirit into your heart and to give you the necessary power and strength, so that you can live as a Christian, so that you can come step by step upward into the fuller stature of a robust son and a fully developed daughter of God who has a beautiful character, who lives a lovely life, and who is true blue in devotion to Jesus Christ.

So you see, the manner in which Jesus met His foes has something in it for us to think about. I hope that what it has been my privilege to say to you this evening will help you, that the Spirit of God will use it and bless it in the heart of each of you.

IT TAKES COURAGE TO BE A CHRISTIAN

"And Simon Peter followed Jesus, and so did another disciple: that disciple was known unto the high priest, and went in with Jesus into the palace of the high priest. But Peter stood at the door without. Then went out that other disciple, which was known unto the high priest, and spoke unto her that kept the door, and brought in Peter. Then saith the damsel that kept the door unto Peter, 'Art not thou also one of this man's disciples?' He saith, 'I am not.'" John 18:15-17.

✓ ✓ ✓

THE Christian religion has been criticized for many different reasons. Some who hold it in contempt profess to despise Christianity because they claim it to be an ivory tower to which such persons flee who do not have the strength to take the shocks and the knocks of life. I am ready to admit that Christianity is a religion of comfort. It is a haven of refuge to which harrowed and tormented souls can flee, but it is not an escapist religion. Christianity does not invite us to leave the realities of life or to hide away from them. Quite on the contrary, Christianity is a religion which invites us to face the harshness and hardnesses of life. Christianity is not a religion for cowards and weaklings. It is rather a religion which calls for fortitude.

If our text of this evening tells us any one thing, it teaches us that *"it takes courage to be a Christian."* When Jesus was first taken captive all of His disciples forsook Him and fled. It did not take very long for some of them at least to bethink themselves, to gather their wits, and to turn about. Certainly Peter and John did just that. It seems they tried with such courage as they could muster to follow Jesus when He was taken to the palace of the high priest. Apparently John was acquainted in that area and so he was admitted to the courtyard. When he had found admittance, he did what you and I would have done under similar circumstances.

He tried to get his friend, Peter, in likewise. And he succeeded.

PETER LEARNED THAT IT TAKES COURAGE
TO BE A CHRISTIAN

Peter loved Jesus. When he promised Jesus that he would not forsake him under any circumstances, we can be sure he meant every word of it. He had no intention of deserting his Lord. There was genuine affection in his heart. Peter no doubt felt toward Jesus as you feel toward Him. You love Jesus, and you would like to be courageous and you would like to be loyal to God, too. But when Peter got into that courtyard, he discovered very quickly that his Christian faith got him into difficulties. A woman, who was no particular credit to her own kind, recognized him as one of the disciples. She pointed the finger of accusation at him and said, "You are also one of this man's disciples." Peter had not quite bargained for such a situation. He had not previously known just how real the temptation to deny his Lord might come to be. But when he saw that finger pointing at him, when he heard that voice of accusation and then reckoned what the consequences might be, should he admit that he was a disciple of Jesus, he could not make it. He was not as strong as he thought he was. He gave the shameful answer which has stood against him in the sacred record throughout the centuries. He said, "I am not."

CHRISTIANITY "PUTS YOU ON THE SPOT"

Just as the discipleship of Peter put him "on the spot," as our boys would say, so your Christian profession of faith will continuously put you "on the spot." If you have the kind of Christianity which you try to hide and no one ever can discover that you even presume to be a Christian, you will very probably have no trouble with such Christianity. But of course, that is not Christianity. Christianity is something which expresses itself. Just so soon as the world discovers that you are a Christian, it will point the finger of accusation at you and say, "And you, too, are one of this man's disciples."

The world of today will probably not say it just in those words. It will have its own way of saying it, but it will say it and say it quite unmistakably. Sometimes the world will point the finger at you and say, "And you, too, are one of those poor, benighted obscurantists who still believes such silly things as miracles. You, too, who live in this enlightened age still believe that Jesus was born of the virgin. You, too, still believe that the Bible is the inspired Word of God." When men begin to make fun of your intellect, when they treat you as though you were a simple child who had not yet seen the light of modern sophistication, you will not like it. You do not like to be treated that way. Such scorn cuts deeply, hurts badly. You will not like it. Or, again, the world may point the finger of accusation at you and say, "What, you still believe in those old fashioned things people used to believe in? You are bringing your children up on such ideas? I did not think any enlightened person still believed in that sort of thing. Why don't you bring your children up as smart people rear theirs and allow religious ideas to take their course? Let them choose, what they want to choose, when they are old enough and wise enough to make their own choices. Why try to fill them up with all such stuff? Why don't you send your children to good schools and never mind that sort of thing?" You don't like to be told that you are a back number. You would like to be right in step with the latest ideas of educators and psychologists. It hurts your pride a bit to have somebody tell you that you are trailing behind the parade of modern thought.

If you are a young person the world may get at you in another way. It may say, "You don't mean to say that you are one of those prudish puritans who still thinks that he should inhibit himself! Don't you know that modern man thinks that the smartest way to live is to live out your life? Don't repress things. It will be bad for you. Do what you like to do. Be free in expressing yourself. Who told you that these things are wrong? Don't be a wallflower. Don't lose out on a good time. Live out your life." Young people don't like to be wallflowers. They don't like to be thought of as back numbers and old fogies. It hurts them to have anybody think that they are of the goody-goody, namby-pamby type. It doesn't go so well, that finger pointing, "You, too, are one of this man's disciples."

Or the world may point to you as a citizen of the world, a businessman, a professional man or woman and say, "What, you mean to say that a person of your intelligence is one of these empty-headed dreamers and idealists who cannot get his feet on the ground and face realism? What is all this nonsensical talk about love overcoming human hearts or the meek inheriting the earth? Who will talk about that? In the day of modern warfare and of the atomic bomb you have to be realistic. Surely you are not going to let anyone impose any such nonsense on you." We would all like to be right in the stream of things. We would like to be hard, two-fisted. So when they point the finger, we are going to say something. Just what are we going to say?

PETER FAILED IN COURAGE

Peter gave his answer. When the woman said, "Thou also art one of this man's disciples," he tried to look her in the eye as well as he could, and he said, "I am not." Probably his voice trembled a bit. Certainly he was deeply ashamed of what he said, but that was the best he could do. He could not face it.

HAS YOUR COURAGE FAILED?

If you think over your life, I am inclined to believe you can think of instances in which you did exactly what Peter did. When the invitation came to go along with the world, to do as others did, well, then you were a good fellow. You talked like the world talked, you behaved like the world behaved, and you said, "I don't belong to Christ." Maybe you did not say it right out in those words, but your actions spoke louder than your words. You did not have to use any words. The way in which you behaved proved all that was necessary to free you from the accusation that you were a disciple of Jesus.

PETER REPENTED

Peter knew just how sad his behavior had been. It was not very long before he was convulsed on the inside. He could not stay in that courtyard any longer. He had to go out where he could be alone with his Lord. Then he gave way to tears as only such an impulsive person as Peter could give way to tears. Some people can cry and some people cannot cry. Peter could cry. He could express in the most eloquent way what was going on in his heart. Oh, he was so ashamed.

My friends, there is a great deal of comfort in it for us, that such a thing occurred in the Passion of our Lord. When you stop to consider how many times you in your own way and in your personal experience have said, "I do not belong to Jesus," not necessarily always by words, much more often by deeds, when you stop to consider that, it surely must be a comfort to you to know that Jesus, your blessed Savior, bore also this humiliation. He suffered a great deal during those few days of His great Passion, but I am sure that one of the things that hurt Him about as much as any other thing that happened, was Peter's denial of Him: "I know not this man."

The fact that Jesus bore this should make you realize that He has atoned also for your denials. If there is something in your heart and conscience which is bothering you tonight, if something you have been doing, something you have been thinking and saying has been a denial of Jesus, then come to this same Jesus whom you have denied. He has atoned also for that sin. Now, no matter how often you may have done it, no matter how grievous the sin may have been and how bold and brazen your denial may have been, come to Christ. He atoned also for that kind of thing. Just as He received Peter again, so is He ready to receive also you. The door to His heart has not been locked against you. He is inviting you to come. He wants you to have in your soul that blessed peace which only He can give.

JESUS DID NOT FAIL

When we observe how Peter behaved himself we cannot but by way of contrast think of the manner in which Jesus conducted Himself. They accused Jesus, too. Jesus would have liked to have been relieved from the necessity of drinking this cup of infinite suffering. He certainly had pleaded with the Father for such relief, but the Father let the whole burden rest on Him and asked Jesus to empty the cup down to the last bitter drop. And Jesus did. He never wavered, no matter how hard the struggle. Even though His soul was exceeding sorrowful even unto death, yet He went steadfastly on to the goal, neither looking to the right nor to the left but keeping His eye on the ultimate objective, the complete redemption of the whole human family, the wiping out of the total human guilt. That was loyalty.

That was devotion to a principle. That was rigid adherence to the way, the will, the plan of God.

DON'T STOP TRYING

If our Lord's suffering should bring us comfort, our Lord's loyalty and devotion ought to bring us inspiration and stimulation. You are trying to live a Christian life. You know better than I can tell you how many times you stumble and fall. You are not making a perfect job of what you have undertaken to do. That is just as true of me as it is of you. But throughout our struggle, in all our battles with the forces of evil we should never give up. The very manner in which our Lord stuck to His task should keep strength and courage in us. This should be the inspiration that keeps us going. We should follow in the way in which He walked. This has all been beautifully expressed by the Christian poet whose words we do well to make our own. He said,

> *"Jesus, and shall it ever be,*
> *A mortal man ashamed of Thee? . . .*

> *"Ashamed of Jesus, that dear Friend*
> *On whom my hopes of heaven depend?*
> *No, when I blush be this my shame,*
> *That I no more revere His name."*

May the Spirit of God help each one of us to make this our personal prayer and determined confession.

THE CASE OF CHRISTIAN TRUTH

"The high priest then asked Jesus of His disciples, and of His doctrine. Jesus answered him, 'I spake openly to the world; I even taught in the synagogue, and in the temple, whither the Jews always resort; and in secret have I said nothing. Why askest thou Me? Ask them which heard Me, what I have said unto them: behold, they know what I said.' And when He had thus spoken, one of the officers which stood by struck Jesus with the palm of His hand, saying, 'Answerest thou the high priest so?' Jesus answered Him, If I have spoken evil, bear witness of the evil: but if well, why smitest thou me?' " John 18: 19-23.

✦ ✦ ✦

THE text which I just read to you affords us a welcome opportunity to consider *the case of Christian truth*.

HOW CHRISTIAN TRUTH WAS REVEALED

We observe when we read this text that *Christian truth is openly, freely, frankly told, and available to all.* It is a truth which God gave by special revelation through His prophets in the days of the Old Covenant and through the evangelists and apostles in the days of the New Testament. He gave it more particularly through the preaching and teaching of Jesus, the Son of God Himself. Jesus spent the greater part of His public ministry in preaching the words of eternal truth. He went to the Jewish synagogs, to the temple. He appeared in the public marketplace. He taught men at the seashore and on the mountain side. He visited in the humble cottage of the poor man and in the more pretentious home of the rich man so that He might everywhere have opportunity to tell men the truth of sin and grace.

This truth has been preserved unto us in a most miraculous and wonderful way. Dean Weigle of Yale Divinity School, who headed the committee which pro-

duced the new translation of the New Testament, de-
clares in the preface to this publication, that all of the
textual findings which have been made by New Testament scholars, since the King James Version was prepared, have made no change in any parts of Christian
teaching. Thus God has not only once given His truth,
but He has wonderfully preserved it so that men everywhere might have it.

The whole Bible or generous parts of the Bible have
by now been translated into a thousand different languages and dialects. Thus has God made His truth
available to all. And equally wonderful is the fact that
He has given this truth in such simple language. We
teach the Word to people of all ages. We begin with the
tiny little tots in the lowest departments of our Sunday
School and in our kindergarten, and though this truth
tells of God and of His infinite love and eternal being,
yet it is told in such simple words that the smallest child
can understand and gain benefit therefrom. At the same
time it is a truth so wonderful that the profoundest
scholar, the wisest scientist and philosopher cannot begin to fathom or exhaust its meaning.

MAN OFTEN TRIES TO CONCEAL TRUTH

This is so different from man's way of doing. Jesus
could truthfully say, "I spoke openly to the world. I
ever taught in the synagog and in the temple whither
the Jews always resort; and in secret have I said nothing." Compare that with the manner of man's doing.
You and I know that some men make discoveries, hit
upon new inventions, and then they closely guard the
secret of what they have found. Instead of generously
and open-heartedly putting it at the disposal of everybody, they guard it so that they personally might derive
the greatest measures of profit therefrom. Think of the
people who bind themselves together in organizations

and declare under oath that they will not reveal what they believe to be the truths which they have found. Compare the love, the warmth of Jesus with any such procedure. "I said nothing in secret. Openly I spoke to the world." Thus, the truth of Christ and of His redeeming love is there for every man, it matters not who he is, where he lives, what his past may have been or what his present position in human society—God has given the story of His love for you.

CHRISTIAN TRUTH TO BE SPREAD

When we consider the case of Christian truth yet further we learn that this truth, which God has so openly given, is now to be spread by those who have it, who have learned it, and who have been benefitted and blessed by its message. When the high priest asked Jesus about the things which He had taught, Jesus said, "Why askest thou me? *ask them which heard me,* what I have said unto them: behold, *they know what I said."* It is the intent and the purpose of God that you who have received the secrets of God should publish them. That is God's way. That was the last thing Jesus laid on the hearts of His disciples before He ascended on high. He said, "Go into all the world and teach the Gospel to every creature." He said to His disciples, "Ye are my witnesses." "Ye are the light of the world." This is your job.

Just what are you doing about it? Your Lord expects that you should tell your fellowmen what you know about Jesus. If the love of Christ has brought peace into your heart, if you know how to find comfort against the accusations of a guilty conscience, if you know the blessedness of communing with God in prayer, if you know what it means in the hour of sorrow to apply the healing balm of Gilead, then Jesus wants you to tell your brothers and sisters in the family of mankind about this blessing. To make it real practical, immediate and direct, let me ask you, what did you do about it today? To whom did you speak today about your faith? We talk about many things. We talk about our homes, our families, our businesses, our golf scores, our investments, our pleasures, but to whom did you speak today about the love of God in Christ? Just what kind of an effort have you made throughout this whole Lenten season to invite even one person to come with you into God's house and to rejoice with you over the message of Christ's love? That is a direct question. Jesus said, He wants people to ask you. You know what He teaches, and He wants you to tell them. I do not think we would have any empty seats in this house of worship tonight, if you had asked somebody. I am sure that we would have every available space afforded by this spacious house of worship filled with persons endowed with immortal souls and brought under the sound of Christ's Gospel, had you told. That is what your Lord expects of you.

CHRISTIAN TRUTH SHOULD BE LIVED

Nor are we to tell others only by our words, *we are to tell also by our lives*. The love which we show for the Word, the enthusiasm which we have for Christ, the devotion wherewith you give yourself to the work in the kingdom of God should be a wordless sermon to a world lost in sin. Our example can be a blessing or a curse to our fellowmen. George Truett, one of the most widely famed Gospel preachers of the southland of our country during the past thirty-forty years, tells in one of his sermons how on an occasion he was in a certain city preaching for a week or more. He noticed on the first two nights that a boy of adolescent age, standing in the rear, seemed to be very much interested in the message. There seemed to be a certain earnestness and eagerness about him. The third and fourth nights Dr. Truett observed that this same boy was deliberately indifferent and disinterested as though he had made up his mind that he wanted no part of this Gospel. The change in attitude was very striking so he made it a point to get hold of this boy immediately after the service. He drew him aside and said to him, "Son, I noticed that on the first several nights you were very much interested and on the past two evenings you have been deliberately indifferent. Just what has happened to you?" The boy said, "I would rather not speak about it." "Well," he said, "I don't want to coerce you, but I do wish that you would tell me because I would like to help you." Then the boy broke down. He said, "I have made up my mind not to join. I have decided that I am going to follow my father. My father is a very successful doctor. My father does not believe in Jesus and does not go to church. I think that my father is a very good man. I am going to follow my father." So the wordless example of the father was destroying the soul of his son. The next morning Dr. Truett went to call on this eminent physician. He told him very briefly of his experiences the night before. The doctor paled and promised that he would do something about it. That night he came. When the invitation was given for those to come forward who would like to accept Jesus and learn more about Him, the doctor came. His son was in the audience. When he saw his father go, he followed. He would do as his father did.

Somewhere in this life and world somebody is watching you. It may be your son or daughter, it may be your wife or your husband, it may be your neighbor, it may be the person who works along side of you in the office or in the shop. Somebody is watching you. Your life, your example is building them up or pulling them down. It is our task by what we tell through our lives to bring people the story of Jesus and His redeeming love.

We also have a marvelous opportunity to do this by showing the world how a Christian is able to meet the crises of life, how he can bear sorrow, heartache, pain, disappointment, and whatever else there may be by way of bitterness in this world. A Christian young woman attending one of our adult classes this season was told by her physician that she needed surgical care. She was quite terrified because of it. She had young children. She was worried whether she would safely come through this operation. She frankly said, "I am very much afraid." I had the privilege to tell her how to use her Christian faith and how by her trust to show that she had a secret source of strength that non-Christians did not have. The doctors and the nurses would have to see from her fearlessness and calm that she was a Christian. When it was all over she told me that during the operation the doctor spoke to her,—she was under a local anaesthetic. He said, "I don't know whether you realize it or not, but you are an unusually good patient." He got the point. He knew there was something in the heart of this woman which enabled her to be fearless. It was her simple faith and trust in Jesus whom she had learned to know.

Jesus spoke openly. He made no secret of His teachings. He did not reserve them for a few initiated people. He gave them to all the world. But He wants them to be given to others through you, by everything you say and do.

The fact that we are witnesses to the world does not mean necessarily that all the world is going to believe. No, it probably will not. After Jesus had said that anyone could easily find out what His teachings were if he wanted to, we read, "And when He had thus spoken one of the officers which stood by struck Jesus with the palm of his hand, saying, 'Answerest thou the high priest so?'" There was no disposition on the part of this man and many others who stood about to accept the truth. Jesus was ready to give them the truth, but they were not ready to accept it. So we must with great sadness in our hearts still testify, there are those who do not want to accept the truth.

Some turn the truth aside because of their pride, their self-righteousness. They are not going to admit that they are helpless sinners. They are not going to admit that they are dependent upon the rescuing mercy and the saving grace of the gracious Lord. They are going to earn their own way to the eternal throne or not win it at all.

And then there are those who do not want to accept the truth because they have some secret sin in their lives. They know that they are doing something which they should not be doing, and they are not ready to give it up. I have been trying for quite a space of time to win a certain man for Christ. We have repeatedly had him in God's house, but he doesn't like to come because every sermon is a condemnation. He likes to get drunk, and he knows that Christianity and drunkenness do not mix. So he would rather put Christianity aside. It need not always be for love of drink. Many times it is for love of money. How many are outside the church tonight because they love money more than they love God I would not know, but I am sure that in prosperous communities such as we live in and such as surround our parish there are many. They are legion you might say. They have one ambition in life and that is to acquire money. The worship of money and the love of

Jesus will not live and abide in the same heart. Finally, a man must make his decision: which means more to him, Christ or material things? The man who is determined to give his heart to Mammon will not listen to the truth when it is given to him. This does not mean that you and I are relieved from the obligation of giving it to him, but it does mean that our testimony may fall on barren soil.

Many other people refuse to accept the truth because of fear. They are afraid of man. They move in a certain circle of friends. They have certain relatives, certain associates, customers or clients who are not Christians. They feel so dependent on them, they are so fearful of them, that they hesitate to come out for Christ.

I do not know what your particular situation in this respect may be. I could not know whether you have honestly accepted Jesus with your heart or whether you have not, but I certainly want to plead with you, if, for whatever reason, you have not accepted Him in the past, then don't do what this man did who struck Jesus in the face. Christ wants to fill your soul with peace. Don't turn it aside. Take it. Take it now. That is why the testimony is being given.

CHRISTIAN TRUTH PROVIDES THE FINAL ANSWER

When you accept this truth you take something that abides. When this rude individual, of whom the text tells, struck Jesus in the face, our Lord responded, "If I have spoken evil, bear witness of the evil, but if well, why smitest thou Me?" Our Lord *could* challenge him. The man had no reason for striking Him. Jesus had not told a falsehood. He had not hurt anybody. He had only told the truth. And the same challenge wherewith Jesus confronted this man on that sad and tragic night is the one which He flings into the teeth of the unbelieving in this our day. If there is anyone who is not accepting Jesus, then why not? There have been many allegedly wise people in this world who could think more profoundly and circumspectly than can the average man. There have been men like Socrates, Aristotle and Plato, and yet when they had done all their thinking, the Greeks still had only a philosophy of tragedy. They did not know the answer to the needs of man's immortal soul.

So it has been with the philosophies of men. The modern world has been devoted to a philosophy of materialism which found its worst expression to date in the ideologies of Russian Communism and German Nazism and which finds a very ugly manifestation in love of physical and material things on the part of so many of our fellow Americans. But what have these false philosophies brought men? This afternoon I sat at the bedside of a very sick old man. I said to him, "Supposing someone walked into your room right now and laid one million dollars down and said, "Here, it is yours!" What would it mean to you? He said, "It would not mean a thing to me." "No," I said, "it would not mean a thing to you, but here comes Jesus to your bedside. He offers you His love, His mercy, and gives you hope. He is ready with His holy and precious blood to let all your sins be washed away and to take you into His arms. That means something to a man in your state." That means something to you. If you have found this Christ then thank God for it. Treasure Him as your dearest Friend, your most priceless possession, and having found Him, tell others about Him.

Perhaps you have not yet made up your mind about Christ. When are you going to do it? When are you going to make the choice? The philosophies of men live out their little day and then they are discovered to be false and deceptive, but Jesus can defy unbelief with the challenge, "If I have spoken the untruth, then tell me what it is, but if I have spoken the truth, then why do you smite me, why do you reject me, why don't you believe in me?" Time is hastening on. The age in which we live certainly is an earnest one, and I want to appeal to you to consider "the case of Christian truth." Make this truth prevail for the good of the largest possible number of people, the glory of God, and the happiness of mankind.

May the Lord be with you and help you play your part for Jesus' sake. Amen.

YES, THERE IS SUCH A THING AS TRUTH

"Pilate therefore said unto Him, 'Art thou a king then?' Jesus answered, 'Thou sayest that I am a king. To this end was I born, and for this cause came I into the world, that I should bear witness unto the truth. Every one that is of the truth heareth My voice.' Pilate saith unto Him, 'What is truth?' " John 18: 37-38.

✓ ✓ ✓

MAY the Spirit of God be with each one of you and enable you to lay down the burdens and cares of this day at the feet of your Lord and to receive from Him, for the strengthening of your faith and the quickening of your love, the truth as He alone can give it.

PILATE WAS CYNICAL. ARE YOU?

Tonight I want once again to direct your attention to the subject of truth. We read John 18: "Pilate, therefore, said unto Him, 'Art thou a king then?' Jesus answered, 'Thou sayest that I am a King. To this end was I born, and for this cause came I into the world, that I should bear witness unto the truth. Every one that is of the truth heareth My voice.' Pilate saith unto Him, 'What is truth?' "

We can almost see how Pilate curled his lip when he cynically asked Jesus, "What is truth?" Pilate was an old Roman politician. He had gone through many a skirmish in the political life of Rome. Pilate knew that the world in which he lived had very little of truth in it. He trusted no one and did not very much expect that any one should trust him. He had not found much of truth on the road which he had traveled, so he was very cynical about it.

Perhaps you, too, have sometimes been a bit skeptical and cynical about truth. We must frankly admit that there are things in our daily lives which make us grow somewhat bitter when someone speaks of truth. I am not so sure that the political world of our day has improved greatly over the political world of Pilate's day. We almost take for granted that persons who are campaigning for a public office will say anything just so they are elected to office. We, the citizens of America, do not even expect that they will abide by the promises which they make. We know that politics make for strange bed-fellows. People who are enemies today will join their forces tomorrow if it means getting an office. Truth is of little account.

We are skeptical about truth also because of the way our daily newspapers deal with it. Even the humblest of folk may be heard to say, "I read it in the newspaper. Of course, you cannot believe what you read." Even very simple, uncritical persons have learned by bitter experience that you cannot trust the purveyors of news. They do not always tell the truth, and if they tell the truth, they often slant it in such a way that it makes for an incorrect impression on your mind. Little children who listen to the radio are inclined to turn the program off the moment the commercial announcement is made. They take for granted that it is not sincere but exaggerated and colored. They curl their lip: "What is truth?"

You and I have repeatedly said within our own hearts and minds: "I wonder what the truth is about the international situation." We would so like to know, just what is the actual relationship between Russia and Great Britain and the United States of America. We assume that we do not know the truth.—When industrial strife engulfs this great nation, we say to ourselves, "I wonder what the truth is? Why has this strike been called? Is it because the employer has been unfair? Is it because of wages? Is it because of labor conditions? Is it because of some agitators who are trying to stir up unrest in the United States and create a situation which will cause us to lose the economic system which we today enjoy? Just what is the truth?"

We find ourselves sometimes asking a bit cynically about truth even with reference to situations which come very close to our own hearts. We know that even in the most intimate relationships of life truth does not always prevail. The fact that someone greets you with a smile, you know, is no guarantee that there is a friendly heart behind the smile. Truth is a very elusive thing. I have known folks who to all outward appearances were very generous toward their children. They probably set them up in comfort and yet did not do it because they loved them. Perhaps they did it because that was one way of extending their own power over these children. So long as they controlled the purse strings, so long did they have power over their sons or daughters. I have seen mothers dress up their little children in great style not for the sake of the children but for the sake of flattering themselves. You see, so false is the human heart, so much is there in this world of what is not true!

This is one of the most difficult things a minister has to deal with in his personal spiritual life. Why am I in this pulpit tonight? I can be here for various reasons. I could be here because that is what I get paid for. I could be here for the purpose of impressing you with myself. I could be here for the sheer joy of being able to engage an audience. Now, if I am true, if my heart is true to the situation and if I am here for the reason for which I ought to be here, then I must be here because I love you and love my Savior and because I want to bring to you, as effectively as I can under God, the message which He has to give. If you think about that a little bit, it should become very clear to you how important it is that a congregation should always pray for its pastor so that he be true and do what he does from motives which are honest and true and pleasing to God.

The human heart is so false and we find this want of truth in such wide areas of life that all of us at one time or another are tempted to say with Pilate, "What is truth?" If you have been inclined to be a bit cynical about truth because of some bitter experiences which you have had, some disappointments, deceptions on the part of persons who you thought were your friends, then let me assure you tonight on the strength and the authority of God's Holy Word that there is such a thing as truth. Jesus said, "To this end was I born, and for this cause came I into the world, that I should bear witness unto the truth."

THE TRUTH ABOUT YOURSELF

Yes, there is such a thing as truth. It is the truth of God, the unfailing, the unerring, the unchanging truth of God. It is the truth of God that probes your heart and that tells you what you are. Our friends often don't tell us what we are. The world certainly does not tell us what we are. The world flatters us or despises us, whatever it believes to be to its own selfish interest. The world has no intention of telling us what we are. It is not concerned, but God is. God wants to open your eyes. He wants you to see how your soul is tainted with sin. This was the thing Jesus tried to impress upon men's consciences. This is the truth which He would like to bring to you.

Perhaps you say, "I know I am a sinner." Do you? Do you realize how fearfully true this is? That is not so easy to understand. You may have some very superficial views about the matter, but are you really deeply persuaded in your own heart that you are in a continuous state of revolt against your Maker? Have you looked down into your soul long enough to see how constantly and unfailingly you oppose what God would like you to do? Let me repeat, it is not easy.

If you have taken it superficially, if you have but mumbled the words, "I am sorry that I am a sinner," if they have not actually impressed you as the profoundest thing in your life, as something for which you really need help, then God's truth has not yet reached your heart. You are still satisfied with yourself. You are not so troubled as you should be because of the real needs of your soul. You do not know how false your heart really is. The way in which we talk about other people who sin indicates that we have no real understanding of our own sins. The readiness wherewith we can condemn others shows what small knowledge we have of our own faults and shortcomings. That is one of the truths which Jesus would impress upon you.

THE TRUTH OF GOD'S FORGIVING LOVE

Then Jesus adds another truth for you. Once you understand what goes on in your soul, once you allow Him to lay bare all that happens within, then He has for you also the truth of God's love. And that is the most blessed of all truths. We often talk about sin as though it were but a meaningless thing. Likewise, we sometimes speak about the love and the grace of God with less enthusiasm than we reveal when we talk about a new home or a new automobile or some other item of interest in our lives. And yet, my friends, I want to say to you with all possible emphasis, this is the great, sublime truth: God loves you. Whatever else may or may not be true, this is a fact.

It is the most wonderful fact in all history. Jesus, the Son of God, became man and on your behalf suffered and died and rose again. He has redeemed you. Let come what will in this world, let the history of humanity from henceforth be long or short, sad or glorious and happy, one truth stands: Jesus gave Himself for you. You can turn to Christ and through Him find with God forgiveness for every one of your sins.

And this Lord who offers you His redeeming love as a fact, not as a theory, as an accomplished fact wrought for you on the altar of the cross, also gives you the promise of His abiding love in your everyday lives. You know that you need that kind of love. Life has its ups and downs. You do not laugh all the time. Your heart is not always bubbling with joy. Your spirits are not always gay and light. Sometimes it is as though great leaden weights were tied to your soul, as though you could hardly drag yourself through life. Sometimes you wonder whether you have friends, whether your health will hold out. Everything begins to look dark. When that hour comes, then remember, one light always shines with an unfailing radiance and brilliance. It will pierce the darkest clouds and bring life and peace and happiness into your soul. It is the light of divine love which shines from Calvary's Cross.

One day a young man came to my study. He had just been released from the federal prison at Atlanta. He was very bitter. He was as cynical as any young man I have ever seen in my life. He was an artist. Some men had taken him in. They had caused him to become involved in some sort of a dishonest undertaking because of which he fell into the hands of the federal agents. The other two men were accomplished crooks. This man was not. So they used him as a scapegoat. While they went free, he was imprisoned.

This embittered him to start with. He had been reared in a Christian way. While he was in his open prison cell where he could be seen by fellow prisoners, he prayed, while they jeered. He cried to God for help. But apparently nothing happened. He began to think that even God had turned against him. Not too long before he was released, he received word that his mother had died—his mother, the one who had been faithful to him, who had continued to trust him even after he was in prison. But yet there seemed to be one ray of hope. Before he fell into the hands of the law he had a sweetheart. As he lived out those miserable days in his prison cell, he trusted that at least she would extend her arms and receive him with love and understanding when he got his release. But just about the time when he was to be set free word came to him that she had married another man. When he came to Chicago after gaining his freedom, one of America's arch criminals met him and invited him to become his accomplice in a life-long career of crime and evil. Oh, how bitter that young man was! Nothing seemed to be true and reliable. Death had taken his mother. God seemed to have forgotten him. His sweetheart had proved untrue.

Indeed many things in life can prove treacherous and deceptive. Human beings can fail us in the crucial hour. But tonight I want to leave this in your heart, the same truth wherewith I could reassure the embittered young man: no matter how lonely you think you are, no matter how forsaken you appear to be, remember one thing, this is a truth, the love of Jesus abides. Everything else may fail, but He will not fail you. He has given you His promise and He will stand by it. He sealed it with the blood of His own veins. This is truth —absolute truth—unchanging truth—about which you never will have reason to grow cynical.

THE TRUTH CONCERNING RIGHT AND WRONG

God also speaks to you in words of absolute truth when He maps out for you the way in which you should walk. He says to you unmistakably, "This is right and this is wrong." We have such an inadequate understanding of right and wrong. We seem to have, in American life today, an idea that anything is right so long as you do not get caught. If you have an income and there is some way of hiding it, you hide it. How will Uncle Sam ever find out? If there is some way of avoiding the law or evading the truth, don't be worried about it, unless you might get caught. That is not God's way. God stands for the truth. God says, "Do this. Don't do this." It is absolute. If you want to walk through life with a firm step, if you want to have quiet assurance on the inside, if you want to sleep calmly through the hours of the night and be untroubled by dreams that haunt you, by worries, by fears, because of the wrongs which you have done, then listen to the voice of God and let Him cut clean for you between what is right and what is wrong. Don't let the world deceive you with its lies, with its dishonesties, its petty thieveries, its gross crimes and sins. Stand by the truth of God. There is such a thing as truth. And oh, how I hope the Spirit of God will give you the ability to accept it.

ACCEPT THE TRUTH

You have not all accepted it yet. Some of you come so close to accepting it, so close to saying to your Savior, "Lord, my Lord, I believe in you. I want to follow you." But just about the time when He expects the words to come from your heart and from your lips you withdraw. Why? Why don't you accept the truth? Why don't you take this blessed truth that Jesus loves you, that He is your Redeemer? Why don't you commit yourself to God and let Him be what He wants to be to you? Why do you run away? When you see Jesus coming down the street, why do you step into a byway? Why don't you let Him take you by the hand and lead you in His way? Why don't you let Him fill up your soul with His love and with His mercy so that you can be one of God's happy sons or daughters? Why quibble? Why hold back? Surely there is no happiness to be found elsewhere! You may have reason, much reason, to be cynical about truth in other areas of life, but there is no reason for being cynical about truth, when it is the truth of God, the truth which He tells you about yourself and your own needs of soul, the truth which He tells you about His love for you, the truth which He gives you by which to guide your conduct as you make your way from the cradle to yonder life and world.

Pilate said, "What is truth?" The world may say cynically, "What is truth?" But as for you and me, let us say, "The Word of God is truth." And may the Spirit of God help us accept it and live by it for Jesus' sake. Amen.

"UNBELIEF"

"Then Pilate therefore took Jesus, and scourged Him. And the soldiers platted a crown of thorns, and put it on His head, and they put on Him a purple robe, and said, 'Hail, King of the Jews!' and they smote Him with their hands. Pilate therefore went forth again, and saith unto them, 'Behold, I bring Him forth to you, that ye may know that I find no fault in Him.' Then came Jesus forth, wearing the crown of thorns, and the purple robe. And Pilate saith unto them, 'Behold the man!' When the chief priests therefore, and officers saw Him, they cried out, saying, 'Crucify Him, crucify Him.' Pilate saith unto them, 'Take ye Him, and crucify Him: for I find no fault in Him.' The Jews answered him, 'We have a law, and by our law He ought to die, because He made Himself the Son of God.' " John 19: 1-7.

✶ ✶ ✶

OUR topic this evening shall be "Unbelief." This is a subject which ought interest us inasmuch as unbelief is widespread throughout the world.

WHY IS THERE UNBELIEF?

When we look at the text which I just read to you, we discover that *unbelief is an attitude of heart, not a quality of mind.* This text shows us *why people do not accept the truth of Christianity.* Sometimes we have an idea that folks do not believe because they find it intellectually impossible to accept what the Scriptures teach. This is not true. It is true that many people in the world do not believe because they do not know what to believe. Hundreds of millions of people in some of the greatest countries of the world are unbelievers tonight because no one has ever yet told them what they should believe. Holy Writ says, "How can they believe in Him of whom they have not heard?" "Faith cometh by hearing, and hearing by the Word of God." We can understand that people who have never had an opportunity to hear should not believe. But when we speak of unbelief this evening, we are thinking particularly of those people who reject the truths of Holy Writ.

59

The unbelief on Pilate's part was not due to the fact that he had no opportunity to know who Jesus was. Jesus had told him who He was. Probably he had heard about Jesus long before this occasion, but if he had never before heard of Him, Jesus lost no opportunity to tell this man who He was, and what he should believe concerning Him.

And surely, the religious leaders of Israel could not plead ignorance. They were very familiar with the prophecies which God had given to His people during the centuries of the Old Covenant. They knew these prophecies from memory. They also had had the opportunity of hearing Christ. Jesus had addressed Himself to them specifically on repeated occasions. They had the chance of observing the life of Jesus. They knew that what He claimed for Himself was supported by the perfection and beauty of His conduct, by the nobility and divineness of His teaching, and by the unmistakable power manifested in His miracles. When Jesus claimed to be the Son of God, as He did, and as they knew He did, they had every reason to believe what He said. And yet, despite all of the information they had, they did not believe. Why not? It was not want of knowledge. It was not a lack of opportunity. It was not because the teachings of Jesus were contrary to reason so that they were utterly unacceptable. No, their reasons were quite otherwise.

No one can read the story of our Savior's Passion without getting a very clear picture as to why these people refused to believe in Christ. The religious leaders had their specific reasons. They did not like Jesus. They had been in the lime-light until Jesus came, but when our Lord made His appearance the masses no longer had the same regard for them. The simple folk very quickly discovered that there was a decided difference between the parrot-like repetitions of the traditions of the fathers on the part of their leaders and the authoritative note of truth in the teachings of Jesus. The people also saw the difference in the life which they lived. Jesus was loving and kind and humble, meek and lowly. They were proud, haughty, and self-satisfied. They stood at a distance from the common man. Jesus associated with him. Hence these leaders lost the popularity which they did not want to give up. When Jesus moved into the forefront of popular attention they hated Him for it.

Then, too, these people were very self-righteous. They had no grave concern about their own souls. They were so sure of their personal goodness. They were the kind of people who never do get decent spiritual understanding. They never learned how to watch at the door of their own hearts to see how much evil came out of them. They could stand proudly in the temple, before the eyes of all, and say with a great deal of sanctimoniousness, "I thank Thee, God, that I am not like other men." People who are so self-righteous have no need for the kind of service such as Jesus came to render. They did not want a Saviour. So it was neither ignorance nor a superior intellect, but rather pride, self-righteousness, envy, hatred that kept them away from Christ.

With Pilate the situation was quite similar although his motives were a bit different. Pilate knew. Jesus told him that He was the King of truth. He told him why He came. Why didn't Pilate believe? Pilate was a politician. He had a job. He was not going to lose that job. He was not worrying about what would happen to Jesus. He was worrying about what would happen to himself. If he would have yielded to that which was right, if he would have allowed justice to prevail, Jesus would have been freed. These religious leaders and their adherents would have been enraged and Pilate would have been accused of treason. Pilate was taking no such chances. He was concerned about himself. He loved the kind of a life he had, the glory, the income, and the power which went along with it. This sort of a thing pleased him. Hence, he was not going to do something that would in any way jeopardize the position which he occupied. So with Pilate, too, it was not ignorance, it was not a problem of the intellect, it was again an attitude of the heart. It was the love of money, the love of power, the love of ease, the love of fame and the most cruelly calculating kind of selfishness because of which he did not accept Jesus as his Savior.

My friends, the point of importance for us tonight is this: as it was then, so is it now. Don't be too impressed when you hear people say, "I cannot believe what is in the Bible. I am too intellectual for that sort of thing." That is not the problem. There is much in the Bible which is *above* human reason, but there is nothing in the Bible which is *against* human reason. It is not true that you cannot be an intellectually honest person and at the same time be a very humble Christian believer.

Very well do I remember the evening, I think it was in the Lenten season, when a troubled young man came to see me. He was in a very bad frame of mind. His head was hanging quite low. It seemed to him that he was losing his job, that his family was falling apart and that there really wasn't anything worth living for in his life anymore. When he told me that he thought suicide was the only way out, I said, "Oh, I don't think so. I think there is another answer. It is given in this book." He said, "Do you mean the Bible?" I said, "Yes, of course." "Oh," he said, "I could never believe that." I said, "Why not?" Then he came with the usual arguments of people who think they have a good reason for not believing the Bible. We dealt with those arguments in a somewhat sympathetic way, but it soon became apparent that his unbelief was not due to intellectual reasons but rather to the way in which he had lived. If the Bible was true, then his behavior was wrong. His whole life was wrong. He then had to accept personal responsibility for the evil things which he had been doing to himself, to his wife, to his children, to his boss. This he found difficult to acknowledge.

A great many folk in this community, like the religious leaders of Israel and Pilate, know what they ought to believe. Every now and then we have the opportunity to tell them in church or in private about the love of God in Christ. But they turn it aside. Why? Because they are so brilliant of mind? Oh, no! That is not it. Some reject Jesus because of complete spiritual indifference. Some of these people are so engrossed with the things of this world that they completely forget the existence of their souls. They hardly know they have a soul. They may live in a beautiful home, but, for all of that, they live like animals. The spiritual is given no thought, no consideration in their lives. They may eat well and drink well and clothe well, but their souls get no food. They are grovelling in the dirt. They are not soaring on wings. Their souls are left out of consideration. Some are self-righteous. They may have a certain concern about things moral. They may reckon with the fact that there will be an eternal tomorrow, but they don't think that they need any help. They never come to real grips with the problem of sin. They just don't dare let their eyes be completely opened to the fact that they are sinners who do need help.

Only the other evening I read an article written by a non-Christian minister. He said, "The teaching of the Sacred Scriptures that man is thoroughly depraved by nature is so atrocious that we can not accept it." Is this his view because he is so brilliant? No. It is rather because he has not allowed himself honestly to face the facts. If he were only a good psychologist, even though not a good theologian, he ought to know what goes on in the human heart. Perhaps he does, but his spiritual pride will not permit him to acknowledge it. Just so it is with some of the folk in our community. They need the love of God, but they may not admit it to themselves.

Then again we have a few in a community such as this who are afraid to accept Christ. They are afraid to come out for Christ lest someone upon whom they depend for business, for friendship, for contracts, for money will turn against them. Their love of money and their fear of man hold them as in a vise.

Sometimes men want to remain in unbelief because of the lusts that are in their hearts. They love sin. They love to do the works of darkness, and they are not ready to give them up. They know full well that you cannot deliberately serve sin and be a Christian at the same time. Naturally, they will not say to you or to me, "I like to be a drunkard, I like to be a thief or a dishonest man so I cannot be a Christian." They will not say that. They will rather say, "I can't believe what is in the Bible," or advance some other excuse for not believing.

If we have any one in our audience tonight who has never yet made up his mind to come out for Christ, to be clean and true and clear in his devotion, in his consecration to his Lord, I want to plead with you, "Look into your own heart. Be honest with yourself. You will find out that yours is the same plight in which

Pilate and the religious leaders of Christ's own day found themselves. Your unbelief is due to your sins and not your mental brilliance. Don't let sin stand between you and Christ, for He is the only one who takes away sin. When you have no Christ, you have no forgiveness. Then you are without hope in life and in death.—Think it over."

What is true of the unbeliever applies also to us, who profess to be believers in Christ, whenever we weaken in our faith. When you, a Christian, act contrary to what you believe, when you doubt God's redeeming love in Christ, it is not because you do not know about it, it is not because there is something in it that runs contrary to reason. It is rather because there is something in your heart which prevents you from taking your religion seriously and from working it out earnestly as before God. It is always sin in our hearts that interposes itself betwen us and our Redeemer.

HOW UNBELIEF ACTS

Our text shows us not only why there is such a thing as unbelief, but also how it behaves itself. Unbelief is exceedingly cruel. Think of it, Pilate took Jesus and scourged Him! Why? Jesus had done him no harm. He was convinced that Jesus was perfectly innocent. Why should he beat Him? This was the way unbelief expressed itself. The crude souls who were in Pilate's court platted a crown of thorns and put it upon His head and put on Him a purple robe and said, "Hail, King of the Jews!" They smote Him with their hands. They made mockery of Him. They treated Him worse than you and I would want to be caught treating a mangy dog. And the religious leaders, these unbelievers, these formalists, who with their lips repeated the traditions of their fathers but who long since had lost the spiritual significance of Old Testament truths, they said, "Crucify Him!" There was nothing more cruel in the world of that day than death by crucifixion. This was the most shameful way in which to die. To have your head taken off, to be stoned to death, these were somewhat more honorable ways of dying, but to hang between the heavens and the earth, to be a victim of the hooting, howling masses gathered around, that was the lowest way in which anybody could die. And it was this, these unbelievers demanded for Christ. "Crucify Him."

My friends, unbelief at no time has behaved itself in any other way. Unbelief always has been cruel. It has always known how to invent and devise new ways and new methods of torturing and tormenting the believer, of bringing pain and woe to the blessed Christ Himself. After our Lord had ascended on high and the disciples went out into the world with the Gospel, it was not very long before the persecutions came. Christian young women were sold into lives of shame and young men into slavery. Christian families were torn asunder. Their properties were confiscated. Some believers were burned at the stake and others were thrown to the lions. There was no torture so brutal but what unbelievers were ready to use it to bring pain and sorrow to Christ's followers.

The unbelievers of modern times, restrained by law, at least in a country such as ours, from resorting to physical violence, have tried by a more refined type of persecution to bring pain and suffering to Christians. Their way of belittling the Christian faith, their way of tearing into shreds the Sacred Scriptures, their way of treating with mockery and scorn everything that is supernatural, has betrayed the cruelty that is in their hearts. And we know that in some lands even in very modern times physical violence against Christians has been fully equal to that endured by believers in the Apostolic Age. Some Christians in our own day have suffered perhaps even more terribly than did some of the persecuted Christians in the days of Peter and Paul.

Sometimes individuals talk as though there were something noble about unbelief, as though unbelievers had an exalted ethical code, as though there were something warm and selfless about the unbeliever's heart. Don't ever be deceived. When a heart is filled with unbelief, that heart is also filled with selfishness and on provocation can become capable of the worst kind of cruelty. Unless the love of God has entered into man's soul and warmed his sinful heart, selfishness, lovelessness, and cruelty will come out. Show me a single place where unbelief has built an orphanage except, perhaps, under the impact of Christian influence and example. Show me a single instance in which unbelief has caused people to dedicate themselves to the service of their fellowmen whether as a nurse or as a missionary or in some other charitable way. Show me a single instance in which unbelief has brought blessing unto a whole people, lifting them out of the depths of dark paganism, ignorance, idolatry, superstition and sin to the heights of a nobler and more beautiful life. Where has unbelief ever done anything like that?

Compare with this the glorious record written by deeds of Christian faith and love. If you must leave your little ones behind, in whose hands do you want to leave them? If you must turn these United States of America over to someone who will keep them for your children and your children's children, to what kind of people do you want to transfer the government of this great country? If you can no longer carry on your business and your children are not yet grown so that they can take your place, what kind of a person do you want to put in charge to protect and preserve it for your off-spring, a believer or an unbeliever? If you were sick and alone somewhere, who do you wish would happen by your way, an unbeliever or one who had the image of Christ impressed upon his heart?—By contrast, as you see, the beauty and glory of Christianity stand out and the ugliness of unbelief becomes so crassly apparent.

JESUS ATONED ALSO FOR THE SINS OF UNBELIEVERS

My friends, the wonderful thing about it all is that Jesus suffered the cruelty of unbelief, that He allowed even a Pilate, his soldiers, and the unbelieving religious leaders of that day to work out all of their scorn and bitterness on Him so that all sins, even theirs, might be atoned for. Even a Pilate had a chance. Even these religious leaders could have found forgiveness. Even these crude, rude, brutal Roman soldiers could have found love and mercy for their sin-stained souls. And there is not an unbeliever in this community for whom Jesus did not give His life.

If you have never yet accepted Christ then see unbelief for what it is. Turn from it. Come into the light of divine truth. Reverently embrace Jesus as your personal Savior. Then light will shine into your heart. Then the sense of warmth and love will come to you. Then a heavenly peace will descend upon your soul. Then you will gain ability to live a nobler life. This love will generate a new power within you. It will enable you increasingly to do things in a spirit of selflessness which will bring you inner joy and satisfaction. It will give you strength to live for the good of human society instead of being one of these poor, pitiful wretches who live only unto themselves, hoping that somehow they will find what they want before they die. No matter how the rest of the world conducts itself, you will live your life with understanding for, and with an interest in, mankind. Your concern will not be only for that shriveled little thing inside of you, but it will be for your brothers and your sisters whoever and wherever they may be.

This faith gives humanity an opportunity for a better world. And if by the Spirit of God you have found this Christ, then cling to Him. Remember all of those little incidents in which you have fallen by the wayside, in which you have made your compromises with evil, in which you have denied some of God's truths, in which you have failed to live your Christian faith out, in which you have been indifferent to the glory of Christ and the meaning of His love, in which you have withheld from Him your gifts, your talents, your energies, your time, and lived as though His cause were not worthwhile. As all of these things crowd in on your conscience and make you feel very much ashamed of yourself, so that you blush, remember, Jesus paid also for all of these sins. He is ready to forgive them all, to take you again as His dear child, to start you off anew, so that beginning, as with tonight, you can live the fuller life of faith, give yourself to Him and to the greatest and the oldest of all causes in this world, the cause of Christian faith and love.

Our choice then must be not unbelief with its cruelty and brutality, but faith, faith in the loving Christ who redeemed us and whose love in turn will give us the power to live a life of blessedness.

A WARNING

"Behold, I come quickly: hold that fast which thou hast, that no man take thy crown." Revelation 3: 11.

BEFORE me I have a group of happy, healthy, wholesome boys and girls. They belong to that generation about which governors, federal agents, prison wardens, parents, and policemen have expressed many complaints. These boys and girls, by the mercies of God, do not belong to the number of those who are delinquents and who have done violence to the rights of their fellowmen. They are here this morning to say to a world lost in unbelief, to say to you as older brothers and sisters in Christ, that they are children of God. They want to declare to the world for the glory of their gracious Lord that they are followers of Jesus. They say this, I am confident, with complete sincerity of heart. They are determined in their hearts to remain loyal and faithful to the vow which they are going to take at the altar of God.

They have about them the assurance of youth. They mean well. They feel so confident, and your prayers and mine go to God's throne of grace on their behalf. We rejoice with them over the confidence which is theirs, and yet, as the pastor of the flock, not only as the under-shepherd of these boys and girls, but of all the flock, I cannot refrain on this happy day from uttering a warning which was first expressed by the Lord. He gave it to the church at Philadelphia, the city of brotherly love, located in Asia Minor. He said to this church, "Hold that fast which thou hast, that no man take thy crown."

SOMETHING TO HOLD FAST

This warning which Jesus gave through John, the inspired seer of Patmos, the writer of the book of Revelation, is a warning which is so sorely needed by all of us, by you, the members of the Confirmation Class, and by all the other members of the church. When the Lord said, "Hold that fast which thou hast," *He evidently wanted to call attention to the fact that they had something*. And this is the truth which I should like to impress on your hearts and minds. *If you are a Christian then you have something*. You have a wonderful treasure. If you are a Christian, then you have a Friend in Jesus. One day I was calling on an old man at a hospital. He was very sick. It was questionable whether he was going to live. A daughter who was present had tears in her eyes as she said, "The boys have not yet come to see father." The boys were too busy making money and spending it to have any time to visit their old and dying father. The old father heard these words. He said, "That is all right. Even if they don't come, I always have One who is with me." That is true. If you believe in Jesus you always have One. Parents may forsake their children or the day comes when death takes them out of this world. So parents cannot always be with us. Children can forsake their parents, a brother a sister, a sister a brother. Friends may move away or they may prove to be untrue. But if you are a Christian then you have Jesus. Then you have one Friend who never fails.

This Friend who will stand by you in every hour, in every circumstance or situation of life will also be a Guide to you. Every day in which we live, we must make our decisions. You must answer from hour to hour and moment to moment: What will I think, what will I say, what will I do? This is right. This wrong. I must make a decision." Oh, what a wonderful thing it is then to have a Friend who is your Guide, who takes you by the hand and leads you to the right decision. David was so appreciative of this. That is why he said in the words of his memorable Shepherd's Psalm, "He leadeth me in the paths of righteousness for His name's sake."

When you are a Christian and Jesus has you by the hand, He will lead you even in a world of such chaos and confusion as the one in which you live. Even in a world in which the forces of evil, the voices of Satan and his unholy angels have an opportunity of impressing us and reaching us so effectively, even in this kind of a world Jesus will take you by the hand and say, "Not over there; over here! This is the pathway of righteousness. This is where you ought walk." What a wonderful blessing to have a Friend and a Guide who keeps you going down the pathways of happiness, of godliness!

But if, despite the Guide, you stumble by going your own self-willed way, and by wandering from that path of righteousness, then, if you have Jesus, you still have a Helper, a Savior who can get you out of your difficulties. When you and I begin to wander from the pathways of godliness, doing things that are contrary to the will of our heavenly Father, we make ourselves very unhappy. Is there anyone in this church this morning who has not at one time or another been profoundly ashamed of himself? Have you never experienced a moment in your life when you felt that you were unclean, when you did not want God to see you, when you did not care to look in the mirror and face the fact that you were looking at a sinner who had a very bad conscience and a heavy heart? Haven't you ever experienced anything like that? Well, if you have, then you have felt the voice of conscience saying to your soul, "You did the wrong thing. You have sinned. You have built a wall between God and yourself. You are shutting God out!" And when you have that unclean, unholy feeling, when you are persuaded on the inside that it is not with your soul as it ought to be, then Jesus comes. If you have Jesus then you have the answer, for Jesus is the Savior who removes this wall of sin and opens again for you the way to the throne of grace.

Jesus is the One who has atoned for all of your iniquities. No matter how great the sins, and no matter how ashamed you may be of them, they have all been atoned for by the blood of Christ. If you have Jesus then you have a Savior. "Whosoever believeth in Him shall not perish but have everlasting life." "The blood of Jesus Christ cleanseth you from all your sins." "Though they be as scarlet, yet shall they be made white as snow." Thus our Lord assures us through His messengers. When you have Jesus, then you really have a precious possession. *When you have this possession, then you have hope.*

God pity the man or woman in this audience this morning who does not have Christ. If you do not have Christ, then you are without God and without hope in this world. Is there anything more sad than to see individuals clutching at a straw, as it were, trying to get some happiness out of the things of this world while they know very well that with every passing moment they are coming closer and closer to the time when they will lose everything? Oh, what a pity to see a great big strong rugged man give all his life and all of his tremendous power and energy, and the use of all his talents and capacities to the pursuit of earthly things, as though these were going to make him happy, when deep down in his heart he knows every moment of the day and the night that with every breath he is coming closer to that point when all that he is striving for must be left behind, when it will mean absolutely nothing to him. Can anything be more sad than that?

It seems significant to me that in these days when money is so plentiful, when people throw it around as though it had no value, more people seem to be saying, "You can't get happiness through money. You can't buy happiness." I have had quite a few persons say that to me within recent weeks. Apparently they are awakening in greater numbers to the fact that this is not the way to peace and joy. If this is all you have, you have no hope. But how different it is when you have Jesus. Then you have hope. Then you are not traveling the downward, the hopeless way into death and darkness, then you are traveling the upward way toward life and light and eternal blessedness, because Jesus is waiting for you. He has prepared for you a place of eternal happiness where you are to be in the presence of God, the holy angels and the company of saints, who will sing His praises throughout eternity. This is what Jesus would remind you of when He says, "Hold that fast which thou hast." If you are a Christian you have something. You have a wonderful treasure. You see, God has been very good to you, you members of the Confirmation Class, and all of you men and women, old and young, who are present here and who have faith in Jesus in your hearts. You have that quiet, simple, trust in Christ. You have something. And now Jesus says, "Hold that fast which thou hast."

A NEEDED WARNING

That was not a gratuitous word. Jesus did not speak it as a side remark. No, this came right out of the very depths of Christ's soul. This was something that was bothering Him, if we may so speak about Jesus. "Hold that fast which thou hast." Jesus spoke this against the background of great experience. Jesus knew the history of His own people. God had given to the children of Israel the wonderful gifts of His mercy and grace, but they hadn't clung to those gifts. They had abandoned them time and again, with the result that only a very few now still had possession of them. Jesus had made a similar experience in His own ministry. When he preached, when He performed His miracles, certain people began to follow Him. He was so happy. Men and women were following Him, drinking in the refreshing waters of life. But there came a day when some of these people said, "No, that is too hard. It costs too much. It is too dangerous. We will go our own way." They did not hold fast to what they had. They left Jesus and went their own way. When we read the Old Testament and the New Testament we observe in how many instances this sort of thing happened. So we can understand why Jesus would say to you and to me, "Hold that fast which thou hast, that no man take thy crown." Hold on to it!

Who would begin to describe the countless instances in which people who once followed Jesus gave up their discipleship. A year ago today, that is to say on Palm Sunday of last year, a man came to me after the service. He had been sitting up there in the balcony. He had listened to the sermon. When the service was over he came and said, "That sermon struck me. What you said applied to me, and from today on I am going to do differently." But he didn't. This man was brought up by Christian parents. He was instructed by a Lutheran pastor. One day he knelt at the altar in his church and promised God that he would be faithful to Him, but he had not kept his promise. He had become so interested in business; he had made so much money; he had become so involved with the people of the world that he was cut off from Christ. I don't think you could have pointed to any one day in that man's life when he sat down quietly, figured it all out, and said to himself, "I am through with God. I am through with Christ. I am not going to be a Christian any more." That hadn't happened, but imperceptibly by little steps, day by day from year to year he had gotten farther and farther away from Christ so that there was no love of Christ, no trust in Jesus in his heart any more. He was a worldling just as sure as though he had never come under the influence of Christ's Gospel. He was as far away from God as though he had been born in the jungles of Africa. He had lost the treasure God had given him. Since last I saw him his name has figured in the news. His wealth has been spoken about. But he is a very poor man because he does not have Christ. He did not hold fast what he had. He allowed the devil to take it from him.

One night I sat with a mature and successful businessman in my study. God and the devil were wrestling for that man's soul. He had found Jesus. "Oh," he said, "I am so happy. I used to worry. My business troubles were getting me down. I wasn't well. I couldn't sleep. I was nervous. I was irritable around the house. The labor situation and all of these things were wearing me out. But now, since I have found Jesus, I am satisfied. I have peace. I know that there is One greater who will cope with these things for me." He had found something. And then there came the day when evil influences began to work in that man's life. They began to dissuade him from faith. The world began to tug away at him and pull him away. Today he is no more free than he had been before he found Jesus. He had something, but he did not hold it fast.

"Hold that fast which thou hast." It is not possible to make plain even to those of us who are older and of more mature years how great, how enormous the forces of evil are. You will, as you go through life, encounter them, one here, one there. The devil does not care how he destroys the soul. He would just as soon destroy a child through the mother who brought that child into the world or through its father as through anybody else. He is not at all particular whom he uses as his agent. And the forces of evil are legion. We have in our own heart the desire for that which is wrong. We have such a materialistic view of life. We are given to mammon and earthly things. We are all inclined to be idolaters who worship the golden calf or the goddess of lust or some other man-made idol.

The ways in which the forces of evil get at us are innumerable. It may be something that happened in your home which sets you against God, against Christ. It may be something which you observe in the life of someone else. Oh, I wonder how many people there are in this world this morning who have said, "I used to go to church, but when I saw a minister do thus or so and so, that settled me." Satan is not at all choosey or choicey as to what means he will use to destroy you. All he cares about is your destruction. That is why Jesus is so emphatic in saying, "Hold that fast which thou hast, that no man take thy crown."

HOW TO HOLD FAST

If you and I, whether we be old or young, whether we were confirmed forty or fifty years ago or whether we are going to make our vow today, if we want to remain loyal to our Savior there are some things which we must do or the forces of evil will take away what we have. For one thing, we must pray.

I do not think I can recall one instance in which a person who had continued loyal in prayer was being crushed by great moral and spiritual problems. It is true, you can pray without knowing what you are saying. I am not speaking of such prayer. But if you honestly and earnestly pray, really pour your heart out to God, the devil will be baffled. He will have a much more difficult time laying his hands on you than would be the case, if you did not pray.

Then the Lord gives us His Holy Word. Just as He enables us to fight off germs and keep our bodies strong by eating good wholesome food, so has He given us the Bread of Life, the Water of Life to give strength to our souls so that we can fight off the forces of evil and live a life of faith and godliness.

Then our Lord would have us be about His business. When people are actively working for the Lord, when they take an active part in the up-building of the kingdom, then they keep that bond between Jesus and themselves closer. Then there isn't such a chance for the forces of evil to come and take the treasure away. People who are inactive, who go to church only now and then, why they hardly notice when the treasure is taken away from them. They are so unappreciative. It is to them not a real living gift from God, something over which their hearts are truly elated. Their religion is purely a theoretical something which they can lock up in a bureau drawer from Sunday to Sunday. When people have such a spurious form of Christianity they don't even know when they lost the treasure, but the person who lives out his Christianity, who is trying to glorify Jesus in the life of man, who is trying to win other souls for Christ, who is doing what he can with his talents, with his energies to build the kingdom of God, to him it will be a living thing, and the forces of evil will not so readily take his treasure from him.

We know that perils exist for all of us and we know that they exist for you, the members of the Confirmation Class. We are very eager to help you. You must pray, you must read the Word of God, devote yourselves to the living of a godly life, and the Church, as your spiritual mother, will try to do her part in helping you. We invite you to come to the Bible Class, to join the Junior Choir, to take an active part in the young people's meetings with a program designed for you. We are happy and pleased to tell you that your appointed class-sponsors will try to give you leadership, hold you together as a class, keep you mindful of coming regularly to God's house and Holy Communion, help you cultivate the friendships which tie you together ever more closely. All of these things the church will seek to do for you.

And of course, as individuals we who are older have a special responsibility. It is for us to show the way. It is for us to live out before the eyes of these our young fellow-Christians a life of faith and of Christian love so that they may see the beauty of it, be inspired by it, and desire then to follow where we have gone before.

This day on which we receive a fine new group such as this into the communicant membership of the church is a happy day in the life of the church. It is a happy day with the angels of God who always rejoice over every sinner who repents and accepts his Savior. It is also an earnest day. It is a day which should remind all of us of the warning which Jesus once gave, "Hold that fast which thou hast, that no man take thy crown." I hope that the Spirit of God will enable each one of us, and in particular the members of this class, to heed this warning so that one day all of us together will lay hold on that eternal crown of victory which our Savior is so eager to give to us in His infinite mercy and love.

FIGURES ON CALVARY

"Then the soldiers, when they had crucified Jesus, took His garments, and made four parts, to every soldier a part; and also His coat: now the coat was without seam, woven from the top throughout. They said therefore among themselves, 'Let us not rend it, but cast lots for it, whose it shall be:' that the Scripture might be fulfilled, which saith, 'They parted my raiment among them, and for my vesture they did cast lots.' These things therefore the soldiers did. Now there stood by the cross of Jesus His mother, and His mother's sister, Mary the wife of Cleophas, and Mary Magdalene. When Jesus therefore saw His mother, and the disciple standing by, whom He loved, He saith unto His mother, 'Woman, behold thy son!' Then saith He to the disciple, 'Behold thy mother!' And from that hour that disciple took her unto his own home. After this, Jesus knowing that all things were now accomplished, that the Scripture might be fulfilled, saith, 'I thirst.' Now there was set a vessel full of vinegar: and they filled a sponge with vinegar, and put it upon hyssop, and put it to His mouth. When Jesus therefore had received the vinegar, He said, 'It is finished:' and bowed His head, and gave up the ghost." John 19: 23-30.

*   *   *

IT certainly is an occasion of joy and thanksgiving to all of us here assembled to know that those of you who were in military service have in large measure already been honorably discharged or are near the day when you can again take off your military uniform and put on civilian garb. We want you to know that a year ago tonight our hearts were not as light as they now are. We rejoice and we thank God that He has spared most of you who were in service and allowed you now safely to be returned again. We are happy that the first welcome given you as a group should be not a banquet in the parish hall but a spiritual banquet at the table of the Lord. I wish that all who were in the service from our church and who have been discharged might be with us tonight. Some cannot be here because they have duties to perform. Quite a few cannot be here because they do not reside in the community presently.

Some are attending schools and some by choice have
been carried to other parts of the country where they
have taken up their abode, but we hope that they, too,
tonight are in God's house in whatever community they
might be.

Gathered then as a reunited family in God, let us
accept the invitation extended by the words of our text
to gather with all the believers of Jesus on the brow
of Calvary and witness the things which there came to
pass when the great drama of redemption came to its
climax. I want to draw your attention particularly to
some of the figures who participated in this drama.

THE GODLESS ON CALVARY

As we reach the crest of Golgatha we observe very
quickly a great sea of faces. There are many people
present and they are a wild, cruel, heartless, and blood-
thirsty mob. They are passing up and down in front of
the cross of Christ with curses and hissing and blas-
phemy on their lips, with godlessness and brutality in
their hearts. A man hanging on the cross, a dying man,
can with bitterness of soul reject the Lord who hangs
at his side and curse Him with his dying breath. Roman
soldiers who had performed the gruesome task of nailing the Prince of Life to the accursed tree were probably the most heartless of all. They were utterly unmoved by the significance of the event. While Jesus,
the Son of God and the Son of Man, is breathing His
last, they are with utter unconcern distributing his garments among themselves and throwing dice to see who
shall get His coat which had been woven of one piece
and was without a seam. This was the last word in
brutality. This was the ultimate evidence of godlessness, of contempt for Christ and for the significance of
the sacrifice which He was making on their behalf as
well as for all the rest of the human family. It really

does not seem possible, does it, that human beings could fall so low, that they could be so utterly devoid of all spiritual understanding, of every sense of moral sensibility as to gamble at the foot of the cross.

And yet if we think, if we make comparisons, we will discover, I believe, that all that happened on Calvary is a true picture of what goes on in human hearts and what is happening before our eyes in the very world in which we live. This is Good Friday. The stock market closes. The banks keep their doors locked. In some communities, great businesses suspend their activities for a three-hour period. Yet, would I be telling an untruth, if I said that the name of Jesus was used perhaps more often for cursing and for profanity in Oak Park and River Forest this very day than what it was used for purposes of reverence, of prayer, and of worship? How did the people of these communities and of metropolitan Chicago spend the hours of this day—looking with adoration into the eyes of the Christ who gave Himself for them, or did they spend them like the gamblers at the cross, selfishly thinking about themselves, greedily striving for personal gain? What was it men and women, young and old, were thinking about in Chicago today, how they would love Jesus; how they would serve Him; or how they would satisfy the lusts of their own flesh; how they would avenge themselves on their enemies; how they would take advantage of their fellowmen; how they would do something for themselves—not for God, not for Christ, not for their brethren, but for themselves? Just think of it, even in the countries where men and women, boys and girls are dying each day from starvation, even there some folks are so devoid of the most elementary feelings of humaneness as to try to enrich themselves by withholding food from the dying so that they might put gold into their own pockets through black-market operations. It is the scene on Calvary, only nineteen hundred years later, not a little bit improved or relieved by those who do not believe.

Even when you and I look into our own hearts we find so much of that same spirit. Here we are in the house of God. Everything is beautiful. All the lines point upward. Everything speaks of God's love and grace, the beauty of His mercy and kindness. Yet, do we love to come? Do we come often? Is this where we center our affections, or is this a side issue in our lives whereas other things engage our minds, occupy our energies and take all our interest and our strength? You see, it really is not for us to point the finger of scorn. It is not for us to turn up our noses as we walk by these poor, cruel, sin-burdened masses on Calvary. It is rather for us to take up our place by their side and in all humility bow our heads and say, "God, that is how I am in my heart. Have mercy. I am ashamed of myself. So much comes out from within my soul which, one would think, could not come out of one who was made in Thy image."

CHRIST ON CALVARY

But these masses were not the principal participants in this drama. Neither were the Roman soldiers and the accusers. The chief participant in this drama of redemption was He who hung upon the cross. Pilate called Him the King of the Jews. The Jews did not like this, but that was not of too much concern. It was not what men called Him, it was what He was and what He did that mattered. See the contrast. While the soldiers were gambling for His cloak, while people were each trying to get something for their own selfish little selves, here was Jesus burdened with the sins of the whole human family, forsaken by God, suffering the agonies of hell in His soul, crying out, "My God, my God, why hast Thou forsaken me?" Still there was no pity for Himself! He was not worried about what was happening to Him, but concerned about all of these people, about this poor man who was dying with a curse on his lips, about the man next to Him who was pleading for help. When this crucified criminal allowed his soul to reach out for help, Jesus responded, without a moment of hesitation, "This day thou shalt be with me in paradise." Jesus' lonely mother whose soul was being pierced through with a sword, she was a matter of His loving concern, "Woman, behold thy son." To John, His loving disciple, He said, "Behold thy mother." His mother should be cared for. And then this hideous group, these cursing, hissing people who blasphemed, who lusted for His life, see how He cared for them. He prayed, "Father, forgive them, for they know not what they do." Down to the last drop of His holy and precious blood, to the last breath that was within Him, He loved them and in love He gave Himself on their behalf. He never turned aside. He never sought for an escape. Steadfastly He went on in the battle against evil, until He could say, "It is finished." Then He gave up His ghost.

WHY DID JESUS DIE ON CALVARY?

What was it all about? Whom did He love? For whom did He suffer? Why did He die? He died for you, you. He loved you. That is why He suffered and died. And it is this love which should fill your heart with comfort. Don't deceive yourself. Don't be cheap and petty and superficial in your dealings with God. Be honest, open-hearted. Frankly, humbly, penitently admit that you have fallen short of God's requirements. Cast yourself headlong on the mercy of your Lord. I assure you, there is no sin so great but what His mercy is yet greater. Whatever may have been torturing, tormenting your conscience, get rid of it. Don't let it haunt you. Don't let it disturb you. Don't let it be a scar which continuously keeps on annoying you. Remove it. Let the blood of Jesus Christ wash it away so that you may be white as snow, though your sins may have been as scarlet.

I should like to say especially to those of you who have been in the service, put your faith in Christ. You have been removed from the ministrations of the Word for a long time. Often you have had no opportunities for Holy Communion over long periods of time. You have been out in a world in which profanity has been a common thing, where the Holy Name of God and Christ have been so frequently and so violently abused. You have been out in the world where temptations are even more violent and fearful than they are in a metropolitan area such as you have in Chicagoland. Whatever your experiences, don't allow the past to stand between you and God. Take hold of this Christ. That is the very meaning of this day. That is why He died for you. There should be nothing that comes between you and your Creator. It should all be taken away.

THE VICTORIOUS CHRIST ON CALVARY

When Jesus said, "It is finished," He meant what He said. Through Him there is peace between God and you. Perhaps we have some in our midst tonight who never yet have come to the point in life where they have honestly, openly accepted Jesus as their personal Saviour. If you are one such, then let this be the moment of decision. Make up your mind, with the help of God, that you are going to trust in Jesus. People so often have strange notions of what it means to be a Christian. They think that they must experience some sort of a sensation which will give them some evidence that now they are converted because they have had a great crisis in their lives. Don't be deceived. Christianity is not merely a matter of emotion. It is not just the superficial flutter of your nerves. No, Christianity is the confirmed reliance of your heart on definite, rock-bound foundations of your Lord's love, on the promises of His forgiveness, on the assurance that He will not cast you aside. That is Christianity. Just put your trust in Jesus. Then you are a child of God. Then the Spirit of God will fill your heart with peace. He will still the voice of conscience. He will allow you to grow each day in fuller happiness and enjoyment of all these blessed privileges of divine love and goodness. Say to your Lord, "Now I believe, I trust." Even though you must say it as once did a man who approached Jesus with the words, "Lord, I believe, help Thou mine unbelief," say it, nevertheless.

FRIENDS ON CALVARY

We cannot, in viewing the figures who are gathered about the cross on Calvary, close without having taken notice of the fact that Mary and other loyal followers and disciples of Jesus were there, too. They were devoted to Christ. Their hearts belonged to Him. The masses were against Jesus. It was not really very safe for Christ's mother and friends to be where they were. But, they belonged to Christ and wanted to let the world know it. Let the world do what it might, they loved Jesus. They believed in Him. They worshiped Him. Hence they were determined, whatever the consequences might be, that they would be with Him in this crucial hour.

Here is a lesson we need to learn. There can be no doubt in the mind of anyone present that the world tonight needs a great deal. We know that the very people who have been responsible for some of the most amazing scientific discoveries of our day are among the first to acknowledge that the hope of the world cannot rest with the physical scientists. We know from the reports which come to us day by day that the world's most select diplomats have not been able so to speak and so to act as to persuade human hearts of the actuality of peace in the international relationships. We know that the hearts of men are filled with fear. They are trembling because of what tomorrow might hold for them. The world always has needed the message of God's love ever since our first parents fell into sin, but at no time in the history of the world has this been so dramatically set forth and made so obvious as in our day. God really is calling to everyone who is a child of His to come out to the rescue of his fellowmen. Good Friday, with all that it means for our hearts and souls, should not only bring us a message of comfort, but also a challenging call to consecrate ourselves to God's service. Mary, John, Mary Magdalene and a number of others, who constituted this little devoted group, should be to us an example after which we would pattern our lives. And it is from this point of view that I would like to make my special appeal to those of you who have been in military service. I know that many men and women who were in military service did not hesitate to pray. Wherever they were, it mattered not whether a boy was alone with his New Testament or prayerbook, or whether anyone else was in the barracks, men and women in military service in the face of battle did not hesitate to gather 'round the chaplain and to send their pleas to the throne of grace before they went to fight and perhaps to die. Many of you have gone through harrowing experiences. You have been surrounded by death on every side. You must have learned what it sometimes takes a lifetime to learn. You must have learned what the power of prayer is, and what the comfort of Christ is to one who might be dead the next minute. God did not let you go through these experiences for naught. He did not just want you to fight for the protection of some material, temporal blessings which happen to be ours as citizens of America. No, God wanted you, as His children, to learn a lesson so that you might become a dynamic force for the good of humanity through the living of a consecrated Christian life. You who have tested the validity of Christian faith and the power of prayer as you looked down the barrel of the enemy's gun, you should be the ones to give us spiritual help and inspiration. It is not for us to give you spiritual light. It is rather for you to give us help, to give this congregation, this community the benefit of what you learned about the blessings of Christianity in time of danger and of battle. Those of us who lived in safety probably did not learn as much as you did.

I want to add that my heart is a bit heavy and that I have been just a little bit disturbed to think that boys could come back home without at once throwing themselves into the activities of the church and not immediately take hold. There may be some men absent, who should be here tonight. I want to lay them upon your hearts. They are your buddies. You can speak their language. Help them!—You know to what depths of moral degradation so many people have sunken in many places. If anyone understands just how sorely humanity needs the story of the cross and devotion to Christ, it should be you. You are young. You have many years ahead. You have all the enthusiasm and the dynamic force of youth. I appeal to you, put all you have into the service of your Lord. Let the church, the kingdom of God, have the blessing and benefit of your wholehearted support, your love, your power.

Jesus did not die in vain. Countless millions have drawn peace from Him and through Him have attained unto life. You and I should gain those same benefits. If you and I will be devoted servants of His, then through us, God granting grace, countless millions of others shall also be blessed. This is the desire of our Lord who died for us and for all men on Calvary.

A LIVELY HOPE

"Blessed be the God and Father of our Lord Jesus Christ, which according to His abundant mercy hath begotten us again unto a lively hope by the resurrection of Jesus Christ from the dead." 1 Peter 1: 3.

✓   ✓   ✓

IT certainly is a matter of joy for me to greet you on this Easter morning. This day has special significance for us, first, because it is the first peace-time Easter in years, and then, especially, because it is Easter, the day which comes to us with a message of light and joy and hope.

MANY ARE WITHOUT HOPE

"Hope springs eternal in the human breast." That is true indeed. But man's earthly hope is very vain and deceptive. Poets and philosophers have observed again and again that "hopes deceive and fears annoy." Anyone who is familiar with the earthly scene of this day cannot but realize how true this is. Who would begin to tell how many millions of people there are in the world this morning whose hopes have been destroyed and all of whose dreams have proved deceptive? I can imagine that there are many young women in war-stricken lands who once dreamed of the day when they could be married, have their own homes, and enjoy the fruits of their labors. But many such dreams have come to naught. Young lovers have been killed, homes have been destroyed, cities have been devastated, and life is not at all as these hopeful maids thought it was going to be.

It is not difficult to picture to ourselves the plight of the Japanese people whose hopes have all been shattered. They were taught from infancy on, that a great day was to dawn for them; that they were a special people of God; that God was with them in the person of their Emperor; that they were the great people of the earth. But it was all a lie. It was not true. Their dreams were not to be realized.

What we see on such an impressive and dramatic scale in these lands beyond the seas, we find in a very definite way also in our own country. Many lives have been interfered with in recent years. Young men who went forth to battle for their country and who dreamed of the day when they would come home to live out the rest of their years in a world of peace, have discovered so quickly that it was not thus to be. They come home, yes, but not to a world that is at peace, but rather a world which is again filled with rumors of war, a world in which men's hearts are heavy, in which they still must wonder whether tomorrow will bring them what they hoped it might. Men's hopes are so elusive, so deceptive, and uncertain that a great many are tempted to abandon even hope.

When man gives up hope, he has given up all. We cannot understand the behavior of great numbers of people in our day unless we always keep in mind that they have no hope. Why is it that people live like animals, that they give way to such indescribable excesses, that they abandon all moral standards? Why is it that so many are driven even to suicide? It is because their hearts have been bereft of every last vestige of hope. They have nothing further for which to live. They can see no promise in tomorrow and, therefore, they are trying desperately either to get as much as they can out of the fleeting moments of the present hour or otherwise to end it all, as they think.

WHY ARE MEN WITHOUT HOPE?

Have you ever asked yourself why this is so? Why should men be without hope? After all, man is God's creature. Why should your heart ever be without hope when you know that God made you? God sustains you. You have never yet drawn a breath without the supporting hand of divine omnipotence. Your heart has never yet once beaten but what the Creator gave it the power to do so. Why should human beings who have been put here by Him, who is the Master Creator of all the marvels of this universe, why should they be without hope?

The answer is plain. Man would not be without hope, if all were well between him and his Maker. The reason why man is without hope is because he has cut the ties that unite him with his Creator. Man is adrift in a world of sin. Man is like a mariner out on the great ocean who has no chart, no compass, no pilot, no rudder, who goes around in circles not knowing whence he came nor whither he is going. This is so because man has chosen to revolt against his God. If we were always at peace with God, if you and I always felt that all is well between our heavenly Father and ourselves, then we would never have a moment of worry. Our hearts then would never be disturbed by a single care. We would know nothing of this restlessness, this feeling of dissatisfaction, this wanting something which we know not where to find. Our souls would be filled with peace. Our hearts would overflow with joy. We would be calm and quiet and strong at all times. The only reason why we worry, why we are so ill at ease, why fears beset us on the right hand and on the left is because we are separated from God. It requires no minister to tell us that. We need read no Catechism to find that out. We have a voice within. This voice tells us, whether we like it or whether we do not, that we do wrong, that we cannot face our Creator, that things are not with us as they ought to be. This has been humanity's cross and curse and burden throughout the ages. This explains why men have at all times and in all places sought for something that would tie them back to God. This is the reason for man's ceaseless, perpetual search for religion.

JESUS RESTORED HOPE

But the very fact that our hearts are evil, that we always fall short of doing that which is the perfect thing, keeps us separated from God. That explains the worry of the human heart. That explains why men have always thought in terms of tragedy and death. And it was because of this, this sorrow in human life, this heaviness of the human spirit, this hopelessness of man's immortal soul that God entered the picture. It was for this He sent Jesus, His only-begotten Son. It was the giving of Jesus which made it possible for Peter to cry out in the words of our text, "Blessed be the God and Father of our Lord Jesus Christ which according to His abundant mercy hath begotten us again unto a lively hope by the resurrection of Jesus Christ from the dead."

God sent Jesus to right what we had done wrong. God sent Jesus to be the burden-bearer, to collect all the sins that tainted our souls and to take that load upon Himself. Jesus came to be the Lamb of God that taketh away the sins of the world. He suffered, He died, He was buried, but unlike man who had to die as a consequence of his sins, Jesus did not remain in the grave. The glory of Jesus is that He, as the Son of God, had the capacity to break the bonds of sin, to atone for the iniquity of mankind, and to come out of the tomb.

Men have been quick to sense the meaning of Easter. It is not an accident that you are ready to get up at an unusually early hour and come to a special service such as this on this particular day. You come, and millions of others in other parts of the world are doing likewise on this day, because the message of Easter has its special meaning. The resurrection of Jesus returns to us what sin had taken from us. It brings us a message of hope. "Blessed be the God and Father of our Lord Jesus Christ, who in His abundant mercy hath begotten us unto a living hope by the resurrection of Jesus Christ our Lord." Our Lord's resurrection gives us an assurance that our consciences once again shall be free. Jesus had to atone for our iniquities. We are told, "There is one God and one Mediator between God and man, the man Christ Jesus." We are assured, "He was delivered for our offenses, but He was raised again for our justification." Whatever the burdens of your heart may be, howsoever guilty you may feel in the depths of your soul, this day's message shall free you from those burdens and give to you an ease of conscience and of spirit which can come only to one who is in perfect harmony with God. You shouldn't have the feeling that you have been cut loose, that you are adrift, that you are lost. You should have the feeling of being tied back to, and firmly reunited with, God, because Jesus has removed the wall of sin and made you one.

If you know this, if you believe it, then pray God that by His Holy Spirit you may learn how to use it. It is one thing to have a theoretical knowledge of the living Christ. It is another thing to know how to use, how to apply this truth so that you may draw from it the comfort which it is intended to give. If you have never yet accepted this Christ, if your soul is disturbed like a seething cauldron in which are churning and boiling the

evils of life, keeping you miserable, making you a very
wretched and unhappy creature, who flits from this to
that, hoping somewhere to find joy and satisfaction, then
don't let it be so in the future. It needs not to be. Jesus
died and rose again so that you can have peace. He
paid for your iniquities. He now wants you to be a
happy son or daughter of God. Oh, would to God that
everyone present here would for today, and all the days
that are to come, have within him, within her, this peace
which surpasses all understanding.

CHRISTIAN HOPE PRODUCES NEW LIFE

When Peter rejoiced so over the resurrection of
Jesus and the hope which this had brought into his life
and the life of all those who would accept the gift, he
spoke of it as a living hope. He said, "Blessed be God
which hath according to His abundant mercy begotten
us again unto a lively hope."

Not only is God in His mercy ready to give you
hope, but He is equally eager, anxious and ready to give
you new strength. All of us have our peculiar weaknesses. We are all beset by one kind of sin or another.
Not any of us can go through life easily serving God
with happy heart and being undisturbed and unannoyed
by the evil of life. We all have our particular battles to
fight. But the message of this day is to make us sure
that we can fight these battles successfully. Whatever
is tugging away at your heart today, whatever force of
evil would like to take you from the pathways of righteousness and throw you into the abyss of ruin and destruction, remember, you are not helpless in the hands
of evil. By the power of the living Christ, you can fight.
You can win. You can rise to a finer and nobler manner of life than ever before you have reached. Not any
of us needs to go on feeling that we are lost, that there
is no hope, that we have become the victims of sin to

such a degree that we no longer can be liberated. No, by the mercies and by the power of the living Christ we can win and God will see that we shall win.

This is something which should give us hope not only for ourselves, but it also should quiet our hearts, if we are disturbed about some dear one. Fathers and mothers often watch with concern over sons and daughters who pass through all the temptations of life. Whose is the father's or mother's heart which has not been concerned about the development of the children? Someone present may have a wife who never yet has come to know Jesus, or a husband who never yet has knelt at the foot of the cross. If that happens to be your particular situation then don't give up hope. Oh, no, we have the assurance of our Lord that these situations can be coped with. We can by the power of the Holy Spirit win the victory. We need never abandon our dear ones to the Evil One and say, "He is lost." Read the Sacred Scriptures and you will find so many illustrative examples of how God has taken people out of the depths and raised them up and allowed them to become a blessing unto many.

This message which is to give us confidence in our battle against evil is also to dry our tears and still our hearts in those moments when we are concerned about our dear ones who have been taken from us by the cruel hand of death. Death is no respecter of persons. It reaches down into this home, into that family circle. It takes young and old, male and female alike. Many hearts each day and each year are made heavy because a dear one has been taken away. Perhaps your heart is a bit heavy today. Perhaps you have been mourning for a loved one whom you miss each day. If so, remember you have been begotten unto a living hope. If your dear one fell asleep in Christ, then it will not be a separation for all time. Then it is not as though you had lost a dear one, for they who fall asleep in Jesus but precede us into the realms of eternal happiness. Jesus said, "Because I live you shall live also." Jesus has given us the assurance that through Him we are more than conquerors. And so one day there shall be a blessed reunion between the dear ones who have gone on before and ourselves who still linger on in this world.

HOPE IN THE HOUR OF DEATH

This blessed truth which gives us cheer and comfort even in the hour of darkest sorrow comes to us also as a source of unfailing strength and assurance when the final call comes to ourselves. It really is a wonderful thing to observe how Christians can face up not only to every pain and grief of life, but even to the realities of death. I have seen more than one Christian die with a smile of victory on his face. Young men, back from military service, have said to me, "Yes, there were times when death was very near, but I was prepared." They knew this: they had been begotten again unto a living hope by the resurrection of Jesus Christ our Lord. This hope, this strength, this confidence, which was in their hearts, and which has allowed many a Christian warrior to meet death unafraid, should be in the heart of each of us. We do not know just what life may have in store for us. I know that some of you are in delicate health. One has one kind of trouble, another, another kind. Some suffer from heart ailments. They realize that life is very, very uncertain. I have a very old father. He has a delicate heart. He knows that at any moment the angel of death might call, but that doesn't take all joy out of his life. When one knows Christ then he can live hopefully and cheerfully whatever the number of his days might be, whether they be many or few. Through Christ the victory still is ours.

"Blessed be the God and Father of our Lord Jesus Christ, who hath in His abundant mercy begotten us again unto a lively hope." Many of life's experiences may prove very disappointing. Much of what lies ahead for tomorrow may be very uncertain. All our earthly hopes may be put to naught. We do not know. I cannot tell you what kind of a government the United States will have when you come to the end of life's road. I cannot give you the assurance that the world's diplomats are going to succeed in preventing another world war. I cannot tell you that the savings you are trying to lay up, the insurance policies you are buying, the money which you are depositing with the government for old age, that all of these things will have value when you should like to use them. I do not know whether you will come to the end of life's road amidst affluence or whether you will be in a poor house. I know the answer to none of these questions. But there is one thing I know: "He lives, He is risen." And because that is true, you and I can say, "Thanks and praise and glory be to God, who hath given unto us a living hope through the resurrection of our Lord and Savior Jesus Christ." None of life's vacillating and ever-changing circumstances shall rob us of this hope. I pray God that every heart here present may be filled with it, that your life may be enriched with it, and that, with the light of hope burning in your heart, you can live out a beautiful life for God, for Christ, for your fellowmen, until you come to be where He is who said, "Where I am there shall my servant also be."

May God be with you, and so lead, guide, and bless you for the sake of the living Christ. Amen.

CHEER UP! THERE'S HOPE

"In the end of the sabbath, as it began to dawn toward the first day of the week, came Mary Magdalene and the other Mary to see the sepulchre. And, behold, there was a great earthquake: for the angel of the Lord descended from heaven, and came and rolled back the stone from the door, and sat upon it. His countenance was like lightning, and his raiment white as snow: And for fear of him the keepers did shake, and became as dead men. And the angel answered and said unto the women, 'Fear not ye: for I know that ye seek Jesus, which was crucified. He is not here: for He is risen, as He said. Come, see the place where the Lord lay. And go quickly, and tell His disciples that He is risen from the dead; and behold, He goeth before you into Galilee; there shall ye see Him: lo, I have told you.' And they departed quickly from the sepulchre with fear and great joy; and did run to bring His disciples word. And as they went to tell His disciples, behold, Jesus met them, saying, 'All hail.' And they came and held Him by the feet, and worshipped Him. Then said Jesus unto them, 'Be not afraid: go tell my brethren that they go into Galilee, and there shall they see me!"—Matthew 28: 1-10.

✻

↗   ↗   ↗

A DAY OF JOY

IT is a sacred privilege to have the opportunity of greeting so large and happy an Easter congregation as this. In the name of the blessed and risen Christ, our beloved Lord, I want to welcome you all. I hope that the Spirit of God will allow your presence to be an experience which will bring you spiritual enrichment and which will enable you to leave this house of God with a measure of love, of faith, of hope, and of courage which will exceed that which was in your hearts when you entered.

This Easter Day we are especially happy because so many of our men who were in uniform are back with us again, wearing their civilian garb, and actively taking up their respective places in the life of the church.

99

That is a more comforting thought than the idea that they should be out on some battlefield in imminent prospect of death. We thank God for their return. We hope that they, too, are pouring out gratitude to the Lord who was gracious and who brought them back.

It is the event of Easter which brings out a congregation such as this, and it is right that it should. You are all familiar, I take it, with the facts of Easter. We need not rehearse them in great detail, but I should like to sketch them for you at least hurriedly and briefly. You will remember, it was on Good Friday at nine o'clock in the morning when Jesus was nailed to the cross. He suffered the agonies of hell in body and in soul. He was forsaken of God. He cried out in His loneliness and hellish pain, "My God, my God, why hast Thou forsaken me." Then at three o'clock in the afternoon He spoke those three memorable words, "It is finished," the most significant words ever uttered in the history of mankind—"It is finished." Then loving hands took His lifeless body from the tree of the cross, wrapped it in grave clothes, and laid it in Joseph's tomb.

The third day after His burial He arose. His enemies had not intended that it should be so. They knew what He had prophesied. They knew what the Sacred Scriptures taught about the resurrection of the Messiah. 'Way back in the Old Testament the prophet of God had said, "Thou shalt not suffer Thine Holy One to see corruption." Even the story of Jonah was intended to symbolize the burial and the rising of Jesus on the third day after His death. God's children looked for such an event. When Jesus was performing the duties of His public ministry He said defiantly to His enemies, "Destroy this temple and in three days I will

raise it up again." They were fearful lest He might.
—He did.

On the third day He arose. The military guard
placed around His tomb by the authorities were not able
to hold Him captive. The forces of darkness, which had
sought to destroy Him forever, found themselves defeated by the sacrifice which He had brought and by the
battle which He had fought. He was the victor. When
on that early Easter morn pious women went to the
grave with heavy hearts thinking that they would anoint
the body of their beloved Friend, they found that the
stone sealing the tomb had already been rolled away.
When young John and impetuous Peter rushed into the
tomb, they were greeted by the angelic messenger who
said, "Why seek ye the living among the dead? He is
not here. He is risen." After His resurrection Jesus
appeared repeatedly to His disciples. John, the evan-
gelist, gives quite an extended account of His various
appearances. You will find it interesting and helpful
to read that account.

NO ROOM FOR DOUBT

If there was one thing of which the disciples of
Jesus were sure, it was the fact that He lives. They
were so persuaded of the resurrection of Jesus and of
the living Lord, that for this they went to a martyr's
grave. One after another was ready to die, rather than
deny that he had seen and heard the risen Christ.

Modern man has been skeptical about miracles.
Modern man has often asserted that he could not accept
what has not been demonstrated in a scientific way.
Modern man has said many things which have been exceedingly foolish, stupid, and preposterous. If it were
actually so that we could believe only what we saw, we
could neither eat nor drink. We would have to deny our
own lives. It is still true to fact that our own life is as

mysterious as anything we know. When modern newspapers tell us that Charles Lindberg and a medical associate managed to keep a little piece of chicken heart alive and multiplying itself, we accept it and believe it because the *scientists* assert it and the newspapers tell us about it. But when *God* tells us that Jesus arose and when men who lived with Him, who saw Him, who heard Him, defied all their enemies, suffered imprisonment, and died as martyrs in confirmation of that fact, and when that living Lord has preserved unto us His testimony and seen to it that it has been translated into 1,000 different languages and tongues, then we still are inclined to doubt.

My friends, the real truth of Easter is, "He lives." "He is risen." That is a fact that is attested to, and that has been in the hearts of countless millions of disciples who have followed in the footsteps of Jesus. If anywhere in this world there is a child of God and a believing Christian, whether he be white or black, red or yellow, whatever his age, whatever his culture, he believes that Jesus lives.

YOU ARE REDEEMED

This is the glorious fact. What does this fact mean? It means a number of things which have tremendous significance for you as an individual. *This fact that Jesus lives means that you are a redeemed child of God.* What does that mean?—James Ullman wrote a book not so very long ago. He called it "The White Tower." The White Tower is one of those challenging mountain peaks in the Alps which every ambitious mountain climber would like to scale. Mr. Ullman describes a group of guests marooned in an Alpine resort hotel. One was an elderly man who no longer had the vigor of youth. Another was an artist, a writer, a poet, a philosopher, but he was addicted to drink. Another was a young woman. Another was a Nazi soldier who was on furlough and who was doing some spying on the side. And another was an American flyer who had been on a bombing mission. On his return trip his motors failed. He bailed out and landed near the same hotel. Thus he became one of this group. Here they found themselves in a mountain resort. Each was harboring in his heart the secret hope that one day he might climb that White Tower. That, each thought, would be the ultimate achievement. And so they revealed their common secret one to the other. One day they gathered their equipment and decided to make the trip. They started out. They had to hurry. Soon the storms would come. And so they went. It was not very long before the old man could not go on. It was not long thereafter when the man who was addicted to drink could not resist the temptation to empty the bottle which he had brought along. He, too, fell by the wayside. The young woman soon found that her energies were not enough to make the last lap of the journey. The Nazi was sure that he would reach the peak, but he fell into a crevice and was lost. The American flyer came closer than any of the others, but he, too, lacked the final strength which it required to get to the top of the peak. They all tried and they all failed.

WHY WE FAIL

This is a parable of life. This is your story and my story. Here we are in this world and we all should like to have an ideal. We all should like to reach the peak of perfection as expressed in the Holy Will of God. We should all like to satisfy deity. We should like to do that which would give us the assurance that we have reached the goal. But as we make the journey, we all fall by the wayside. Our weaknesses prevent us from

reaching the goal. Our jealousy, our temper, our envious heart, our greed, the lusts that burn within us,
our indifference toward things spiritual, our common
disregard for the happiness and the well-being of our
fellowmen, all of these things together in one way or
another cause every last one of us to fail of reaching the
mountain peak. We do not get there. We fall by the
wayside.

ENTER — DIVINE MERCY

This has been the distressing experience of man all
through history. It is because of this falling short that
men have always looked for some way by which they
could get to that peak. All these failures represent the
sins that are in your heart and in my heart, the things
that keep us from reaching the perfection that would
give us inner peace. And it is at this point now, where
you and I fall by the wayside, that God enters the picture and in His own infinite love sends Jesus to be our
Savior, not merely to walk before us and to say to us,
"Come, come. Do as I do!"—but to take us in His arms
and to carry us to that mountain peak, to do for us, what
we do not have the capacity to do for ourselves. Jesus
doesn't stand up there on a pinnacle and taunt us and
twit us and say, "Come, do this!"—all the while knowing that we cannot do it. No, He is our Redeemer. He
is the Lamb of God for sinners slain. He was delivered
for our offenses. He bore our sins in His own body
on the tree. That is why He came. That is why He
gave His life. And so this day, you see, on which we
commemorate the resurrection of Jesus, this demonstra-
tion of His complete victory, is such a day of joy for us.
You will not understand Easter joy unless you take this
redeeming love of Christ and make it the hope and the
treasure of your own life and heart.

DON'T MISS YOUR OPPORTUNITY

And oh, how I want to plead with you in this solemn hour to take this Christ. Some folks hear about Jesus, but, having heard, they go their way. It means absolutely nothing to them. They turn Him aside as though they had seen something which interested them for a moment but upon which they can again turn their backs with complete indifference. May God in His infinite mercy allow no heart to go out from this house of worship without having accepted Christ as its Savior from sin. I want to ask you, how are you going to get to the top of the White Tower unless Jesus puts you there? Is there any one in this audience who thinks that he will be the one who will reach the tower when man never yet in history has made it? Why have men looked for a religion, why have they been looking for somebody who will help them, who will work out their salvation, who will tie them back again to God? Only because they have known that they could not do it by themselves. "There is one God and one Mediator, peace-maker, between God and man, and that is the man Christ Jesus." There will be no peace in your heart between you and God unless you accept this Christ. When He is your Friend, when He does so much for you, then why wouldn't you accept Him? Are you so proud that you want to turn Him aside? Or are you ashamed to accept Him now? Should a man who has been a drunkard be ashamed to become sober? Should a man who is an adulterer be ashamed to live a clean and decent life? Should a man who is not a believer in Jesus, who has not come out before the world and said, "I believe in Jesus as my Redeemer," should a man like that be ashamed to come out and say to his fellowmen, "I did not believe, but I now have found Christ. I am proud of my Lord." Is there any one in this audience who

would be afraid, who would be ashamed so to confess his
Lord who died for him and rose again? God forbid!

DON'T BE AFRAID OF DEATH

Acceptance of Jesus does not only mean that you
get a sense of forgiveness so that you can live calmly,
sleep quietly and peacefully because you always know
that the omnipotent God is your Father who loves you
and who for Jesus' sake has forgiven all of your sins
and transgressions, but it *also brings you the answer to
death*. Death is still the grim reaper. With all the
modern discoveries in the realm of science and the pro-
longation of the life of man, death still looms up ahead.
He is the king of terrors. He reaps where he will without asking any questions of us. Death—that is the one
thing that brings terror to the human heart. Sometimes
you hear people talk as though they did not care whether
they died. The boys in military service were more honest. They did not try to make people believe that they
were not afraid. They were honest enough to say, "We
were terrified!" The cold fear of death came upon them
and they could keep themselves spiritually calm on the
inside only when they knew that they were prepared for
death. Even the boys who were prepared still felt a
peculiar sense of fear in the face of death. But if your
heart is to get courage, if you want to face that grim
reaper when he comes to you, you can do so only with
confidence and hope, if you have faith in the risen Christ
who was delivered for our offenses and raised again for
our justification. Jesus says, "I am the Resurrection
and the Life. He that believeth in me, though he were
dead, yet shall he live, and he that liveth and believeth
in me shall never die." Jesus gives us the assurance,
"Because I live, ye shall live also."

HOW — IF NOT THROUGH CHRIST?

How will you meet death, if you do not have Christ at your side? Whom are you going to trust for eternal life and salvation, if it be not Jesus? "There is no other name under heaven given among men, whereby we must be saved." There is no one in history who has overcome death except Jesus Himself. It is only as you accept the victory which He has won for you, which He wants to lay right into your heart and into your lap, it is only as you accept this that you can have the answer to the whole question of death.

Death concerns us not only when it raps at our door, but also when it calls our dear ones. That is one of the tragic moments in life when one who is very dear to you has been called away. I have seen many people die, very poor people and people who have been successful and prosperous. When death came, it came. They were not able to stay its cold, destructive hand. I have seen little children die who by well-to-do parents were provided with everything the medical profession could afford. Yet they died. And there are few experiences in life which affect our hearts quite so profoundly as does the death of a dear one. I am sure we have folks here this morning who since last Easter were called upon to accompany the mortal remains of some dear one to their last earthly resting place. I know we have wives and mothers in our congregation whose loved ones have given their lives for their country and who are not going to come back. What is to dry their tears? What can bring joy and comfort to such sorrowing hearts? Only the knowledge that our dear ones live, only the knowledge that there shall be a blessed reunion, and for this we have only the assurance which Jesus gives.

When we fall asleep in Jesus then we close our eyes on earthly scenes, but we also open them on the heavenly and eternal. What a wonderful thing to be able to know that by the resurrection of Jesus your dear ones have preceded you into the realms of glory to be in the presence of God and in the company of all the great men and women of God who have gone on before and who spend eternity singing the praise of Him who made you. When you so think of your dear ones then your hearts grow light. Then you know that they are not dead, but that they are where all their tears are wiped away, where there is fullness of joy and where there are pleasures forevermore. I certainly hope that the Spirit of God will let this truth soothe your heart and give you cheer so that despite your loneliness you still can go on with strength and purpose.

LIFE IS WORTHWHILE

The story of our Lord's resurrection should not only give us the answer to death and to eternity, but it should *be unto us also a lively hope.* That is what Peter said when he addressed the Christians in days of sorrow and persecution. He said, "Blessed be the God and Father of our Lord Jesus Christ, which according to His abundant mercy hath begotten us again *unto a lively hope* by the resurrection of Jesus Christ from the dead." Through the resurrection of Jesus we are to be restored, we are to be renewed, regenerated, to become new people who are capable of living new lives. This is something. Mark this.

YOU CAN GROW

So often we encounter individuals in life who hopelessly accept themselves for what they are. Whatever their particular weakness of character may be, they assume that is the weakness wherewith they must go through life. They have no idea that it is possible for a man to rise, to put down his weaknesses, to become a new person. Yet, the Sacred Scriptures give us any number of instances in which people who had lived on the lowest moral levels were elevated to the heights of moral victory. Many of you know from your own experiences in life how wonderful this is, how from day to day men can grow, lay hold of greater spiritual power, and attain to higher rungs on the ladder of moral living. You, too, can go onward and upward and become a nobler son, a more beautiful daughter of God. You know your weaknesses, you know whether you have an ugly temper, a bitter tongue, a jealous disposition, a lusting heart, whether you are devoting all of your life to the accumulation of money· You know what your weakness is. Don't accept it as a permanent handicap. Fight it. You can. St. Augustine once was a wastrel who blasphemed and desecrated God, violating every law of decency and chastity. One day, however, God laid hold of him, recreated him and made of him one of the great church fathers. God is doing similar things today. Every Christian minister can tell how one day he picked up some person who was devoted with his whole heart to the service of sin and saw him transformed into a Christian. This is one of the rewarding aspects of the Christian ministry. You can stand in a pulpit such as this and see Sunday after Sunday how this one and that one grows in grace and all things spiritual. What God does for others, He is able and ready to do for you. You are no greater problem for the Spirit of God than any other. So take Jesus. He lives· He lives for you. He wants the power of His Spirit to be a living power within your heart and life.

A BETTER WORLD

And, my friends, *all of this* which has such specific personal meaning for us also *has significance for all of human society.* Human society is in a rather bad way this morning. We don't even have peace within the borders of our own country to say nothing of peace with other nations of the world. Some of the people who were our allies during the past war are today our threat for the next world war. I do not mean to make propaganda for that kind of an idea, but you read about it every day in the newspapers. It isn't a new thought. Are we going to allow men to go on hopelessly destroying themselves? Is that what we are going to wait for? Wait until people become so agitated? Wait for someone to make a bomb and drop it on us? Or do we want to be the aggressors and see that we destroy others before they destroy us? Do we live in a world where people think that there is no hope, where they have no regard for the moral Law? Many of our boys have told me that some of the peoples of Europe have given up almost all morality. How can human society go on as human when humans live like animals and no longer respect the moral will of their Creator? That is not possible.

Think of the situation in which we find ourselves in our own land. Homes are being broken by the thousands. The sacred bonds of marriage are being ruthlessly torn asunder. Juvenile crime has grown apace. We are told by a reputable newspaper reporter in one of our daily newspapers that he roved the campus of our own great state university and there talked to men about the morals which prevailed. They said, "When you see a boy or a girl you cannot tell them apart by their dress because the women wear slacks. To tell the difference you tell a dirty story. If they blush you know it's a man." Just think, my friends. If such a thing should be only partially true what evil it augurs for the future of our country. If the women who are to be the wives and the mothers of tomorrow have no fear of God, no sense of decency, then how can we have a strong United States? We are worrying about enemies *on the outside*. I am not worrying about them. I am worrying about enemies who are *on the inside*, the people who disregard everything that is right and who with abandon, shamelessly and unblushingly give themselves to everything that is wrong. Well, what are we going to do about them? Sing our Jeremiads, give expression to our lamentations and then fold our hands? What did we do about it when mighty military powers declared war on us? Did we lay down and say, "We might as well capitulate?" We did not. We mustered our forces and put our minds to work. We began to pray. We worked. We sacrificed. We sent the finest flower of American manhood to battle for us. We put into this gigantic struggle everything that we had. And thus we won. This morning in the name of the living Christ I want to issue a challenge to you. Instead of standing idly by and seeing human society degenerate round about us, I call you in the name of Jesus Christ to a holy war on the forces of evil. I want to give you a program for action.

PROGRAM FOR ACTION

First, *accept Jesus for yourself*. How is it possible for any man or woman to live in these United States to enjoy all the blessings of divine goodness which are ours, and not accept and revere the God who gives them? My friends, I call on each of you as an individual to make your peace with God. Accept Jesus as your Captain, join His army and swear loyalty to Him.

Secondly, let us *engage in a preventive program*. We Americans think we are so wise. We talk about our efficient methods of production in business, but we allow millions of boys and girls to grow up without any moral and spiritual instruction. After many of them have become criminals, we send the police to apprehend them. Then we try them in the courts of our costly judiciary system, whereupon we often put them into penal institutions where we pay to house and clothe and feed them. So we literally spend billions of dollars every passing year to suppress something which we should have prevented. This morning I want to call on you in the name of the living Christ to give yourself and all that you have to a preventive program. That is what this church stands for. We do not have this church here merely to suit our fancy. This church is trying here to grow a rose, the sweet fragrance of which should carry into the life of every boy and girl, man and woman in these areas. We are carrying this work on so that boys and girls can learn that they are made by God, that they have a Savior who died for them and rose again, and that they are here to do for others so that they might glorify the Lord who has atoned for them. I invite everyone of you to have a part in this work. I don't see how men and women who think can pass by this house of God and not say, "I must have a part in this work because it is not only the Christian thing but it is the smart, the economical thing to do." Why not spend millions to prevent rather than to spend billions to try to correct?

The third point in this program is *an invitation to you to participate.* Many persons are set in their ways. They are not going to come to our church services. Hence, we must reach them in another way. Do something about it. Accept Jesus for yourself and then become one witness for Christ. *You* do this. Oh, we have so many men and women here this morning who can exert a tremendous influence. We have doctors, dentists, lawyers, engineers, manufacturers, merchants, representatives of labor and of management, people in various stations of life. They are all here. You in your particular spot, you should tell men about your faith. Testify. Tell men what faith in Jesus is doing for you. Invite them to accept Him. He will mean the same thing to them. If you, in your place in life, will become a witness for Christ you can bring joy to others and be a great benefactor to society. It is not so terribly long ago when a leader in a great American industry said to me, "Isn't it too bad that the masses are being reached by all kinds of subversive propaganda but not by the message of the church?" See if you cannot find a place in your business where the note of Christ's love and Christian morality can be introduced so that its positive, saving and uplifting influence will make itself felt.

Besides your personal testimony, Jesus would have you use other agencies to spread the Gospel. We have the opportunity of coming into the privacy of people's homes by means of the radio. We can send them Bible tracts, so that they may read the story of Christ. Don't you want a part in this work? Do you want the world to go to the eternal bow-wows when you might do something about saving it! Are you going to let it go, or are you going to have a part in Christ's great program of salvation?

DON'T BE A PESSIMIST

Perhaps you are saying to yourself: "What good will all this do? What can we achieve? What will come of it all? This is a lot of meaningless oratory. Another Easter sermon is over and the world goes on unchanged." Are we going to stand by and let the hearts of men be filled with fear on which hatred, wars, atheis-

tic Communism and all the other progeny of evil are
feasting? Are we going to let bitterness encircle the
globe? Is that what we must do? Should we really
lay down and give up or should we do as we did in the
World War, attack and do our task? Just how tremendous the influence of men can be we can see. There
was a night when a man called Hitler sat in a beer
parlor with a few old cronies drinking beer and plotting for tomorrow. Think what came of that plotting,
—a mighty army which became a curse to the whole
human family. Think of it! So tremendous can the
power of a few people be for all mankind. My friends,
if a few men, plotting with the devil, can become a curse
to the whole human family, shouldn't you and I then,
planning with the living Christ who arose, who sits at
the right hand of the Father, shouldn't you and I, meeting in the house of God, shouldn't you and I, by the
power of God, be able to become a blessing to our homes,
to our businesses, to our community, to our country, to
our fellowmen, wherever they might be? If some men
can plot for evil, why then shouldn't you and I in the
fear of God plan for that which is right and which is
good? So I invite you! If there are any with us whose
hearts are touched, if you would like to talk about this
with me I certainly would be happy to meet with you at
the close of this service or get a telephone call from you
to meet with you at your convenience. It is not enough
merely to go to church on Easter Sunday, to put a dime
or a dollar on the collection plate and then feel that you
have done your duty by God, yourself and human society. No. You must give yourself. You must take
Christ into your heart and with Christ you must wage
war on that which is evil. If so we will do, if we will
take the torch handed us by our resurrected Lord, then
one day we will be able to say not only on the basis of
divine revelation but also on the basis of personal ex-

perience, "Thanks be to God which giveth us the victory through our Lord Jesus Christ."

May God be with us to that end for Jesus' sake. Amen.

THE WILLING CHRIST

"Then said Jesus unto Peter, 'Put up thy sword into the sheathe: the cup which my Father hath given me, shall I not drink it?' "— John 18: 11.

✦ ✦ ✦

ASH WEDNESDAY marks the beginning of another Lenten Season. God willing we hope to gather here each Wednesday evening throughout this consecrated period to meditate upon the passion of our blessed Lord. We have done this in the past. I hope and pray that by the mercies of God we will do so this season not merely as a gesture to honor an age old custom, but rather to deepen our spiritual lives, to improve our Christian conduct, to enrich our personal happiness, and to bless our fellowmen.

If this is to be accomplished it will require prayer. So I would like to urge upon you to pray.—Pray that God may permit me to preach His Word with power and with effectiveness. Pray that God may be with you so that you may receive with understanding heart and appreciative soul His message of love and of forgiveness. Pray for those of your fellow members in Grace Church whose faith is very weak and whose love at best is but luke warm, and who with so much carelessness neglect the means of grace. Pray for those who may come to worship with us, but who never yet have seen the true meaning of Christ. Pray that the Spirit of God may be as a flaming fire in our midst igniting the light of faith and of love within each individual heart so that when the Lenten season will have passed, it will have left a deep and abiding mark in the life of each of us.

How I wish that I might, by the grace of God, engrave upon each heart the image of this Christ who gave Himself for us so that wherever you are, whoever you are, that image might always be before the eye of faith and serve you as an unfailing source of comfort, as a mighty force of inspiration, and as a fountain of strength out of which will flow courage and ability wherewith to meet the problems of life and the temptations of the world, the devil, and your own flesh. As we proceed we want our thoughts to center on "The Christ of Our Salvation." That shall be our general theme. This evening we want to see the Christ of our salvation as "The Willing Christ." Our topic is based on a statement of John.

John tells in the eighteenth chapter of his Gospel how Jesus left the upper room with His disciples after He had instituted the Holy Supper. With them He crossed the Kedron valley and went to the Garden of Gethsemane where He so often before this time had bent His knees in prayer. When He reached Gethsemane the forces of hell were unloosed upon Him. His soul was exceeding sorrowful even unto death. While the invisible forces of evil were engulfing Him, the visible foe came nigh, lead by Judas, one of our Lord's own apostles. When Peter saw what was coming to pass, he, with his usual impetuosity, reached for his sword and began to lay about him. Jesus then told him to put the sword back into the sheathe and asked of him this question: "The cup which my Father hath given me, shall I not drink it?"

THE CUP OF SORROW

The cup—what kind of a cup was it? A cup of joy or a cup of sorrow? Look into the cup and you will know very quickly, as Jesus knew. It was not a cup of joy, but a cup of woe, of sin, of death. When you look into that cup you find things there which came from you. You put them there. It is a cup of poison, brewed out of the evil things which you have done in life. There you find those words which you have spoken but which you should not have spoken,—the words that were unclean, irreverent, profane, untrue, slanderous, the words that were spoken in a fit of temper, words of anger, words that hurt. They are all there. In this cup you find the thoughts which went through your mind and which should not have gone through your mind, thoughts of pride, of selfishness, of suspicion, of revenge, of uncleanness, thoughts of rebellion against God, thoughts of idolatry. These are the things which have gone into the filling of this cup. It is a cup of poison, and you filled it with that poison.

This is the cup which Jesus was to drink. You and I cannot stand by and see that cup and be conscious of its content without feeling a blush of shame. We must bow our heads. Our souls must tremble at the thought that we have concocted for the Son of God who became the Son of Man the cup of death.

Jesus says, "The cup—the cup which my Father hath given me to drink." Jesus knew what was in that cup. The Father knew what was in that cup. The Father also knew that you and I should have drunk it. But it was a cup of death, and the Father did not want us to die. Hence He resolved in eternity upon a plan by which He would relieve us of the cup and have His Only-begotten drink it for us. So He sent Jesus. Instead of letting each of us drink the cup to our own destruction, He took what should have been in the individual cups of us all and put it into one cup and gave it to Jesus. This is love, infinite love. This is mercy, God's mercy, for us poor sinful creatures.

You can never be the happy, blessed son or daughter of God which your Creator wants you to be until you realize and believe that God has taken all the sins out of your cup and put them into Christ's cup. So long as you still stand on the highway of life, holding with trembling hand that cup filled up with your sin and guilt, so long must you be a wretched and unhappy being. It is not until you allow God in His love to relieve you of that cup and put it into the hands of Christ that a genuine feeling of peace can descend upon your soul. Only then can you experience that relief which God would give to you.

JESUS ACCEPTED THE CUP

When God handed this cup to Jesus, the eternal weal and woe of the whole human family were trembling in the balance. The question was, what would Jesus do with that cup? Would He push it aside, or would He take firm hold of it and say, "I will drink it?" It was a tremendous ordeal for the Savior. He cried to the Father about it. He prayed not once but repeatedly, "Father, if it be Thy will take this cup from me." It was not a simple and easy task. His apostles had advised Him to have nothing to do with the cup. They had said in effect, "Stay away from Jerusalem. Stay away from Gethsemane. Stay away from your enemies. Don't go there." But Jesus had gone. And now, once again, when the cup was being put into our Lord's hands, Peter came with a sword. It was then Jesus asserted Himself. He said, "The cup which my Father hath given me, shall I not drink it?"

The die was cast. The mind of Jesus was made up. His whole heart and will were dedicated to the task. You should not drink that cup; I should not drink that cup; He would drink it. He would die, so that you and I might live.

YOUR COMFORT

This is the glorious story of Lent. This is the message brought to us by the Christ of our salvation. Here you see your willing Lord put Himself into your place. He is called upon to suffer infinitely, to die innocently, but He does it. There is not a note of rebellion in His heart. "If this is God's plan, if this is the Father's will, if this is what humanity's salvation depends upon, I will drink it," He says. And so He does. Down to the last bitter dregs, He empties the cup. No sin is left unatoned. Every guilt is wiped out. Every transgression is taken care of and made good, because Jesus empties the cup. This should make you happy. This should take all of the turmoil out of your soul. All your worries should be gone. These deep lines and heavy furrows, wipe them out. Look up to God and smile, because God loves you. All your sins have been taken care of.

Oh, if only the Spirit of God would allow that truth to take hold of every heart here present. If only God's Holy Spirit would give us the ability to apply that truth to every part of our lives. If only from early morn till late at night we could keep it in the front of our minds, how different our lives would be. All of those things that weigh us down would be gone. All of those moments of troubled mind and heavy heart would be no more. We would be happy in Christ, and the peace which surpasses all understanding would abide with us. May God in His infinite mercy grant this gift to each of us as we come to understand the blessed meaning of these wonderful words, "The cup which my Father hath given me, shall I not drink it?"

THE INNOCENT CHRIST

"Pilate then went out unto them, and said, 'What accusation bring ye against this man?' "—John 18: 29.

✦ ✦ ✦

WE want to go on this evening with our meditation on the general theme, "The Christ of our Salvation." Our specific topic shall be, "The Innocent Christ." It is based on the question which Pilate addressed to the accusers of Jesus, concerning whom we read: "Pilate then went out unto them, and said, 'What accusation bring ye against this man?' "

A DARK NIGHT

It was one of the darkest nights in history. All the forces of darkness were unloosed. They were determined to work out their hellish purposes and their demonic hatreds against Christ, the Holy One of God. Led by a traitor, they went to the Garden of Gethsemane. They took Jesus captive, bound Him, and brought Him first to Annas and then to Caiaphas, the active high priest of that season. The members of the Sanhedrin, which was the supreme court of the Jews, assembled, and Jesus was made to appear. He should have enjoyed every advantage of a fair and just trial. The rules of procedure followed by this court ordinarily represented the very highest standards of justice, of truth, and of humanity. But this night, this very dark night in history, also the standards of justice which ordinarily prevailed in this court were put into the discard, and Jesus was condemned. Right or wrong, guilty or innocent, He was condemned, and early the next morning they took Him off to Pilate, the Roman governor and judge.

They brought Him to Pilate because they wanted Him killed. Rome had taken the power over life and

death from the supreme court of the Jews, and so, for
the attainment of their purposes, they had to go to
Pilate. These people were the religious leaders in Israel.
They were the outstanding members of the organized
church in that day. If anyone in all the world should
have been able to understand and appreciate the significance of Jesus, it should have been they, but they
did not. They hated Him. They rejected Him. They
were determined to kill Him, and so they insisted, He
must die.

<h2 style="text-align:center">OTHER INSTANCES OF DARKNESS</h2>

If this had happened only once in history, if only
on one very dark night throughout the story of mankind
there had been a band of mobsters who in a wild frenzy
had lost all their senses and demanded the death of
Jesus it would be understandable, even if it would not
be excusable. But, unfortunately, that was not the only
time. This hatred, this bitterness, this rejection of Jesus
has continued from that day to this.

Jesus said, "I am the Son of God. The Father and
I are one." His enemies said, "You are a liar. You are
a blasphemer. You are not the Son of God." They said
it when they took Jesus to Pilate. They said it in the
years following the Apostolic Age when Athenasius had
to wrestle with Arius in order to preserve the truth of
the true humanity and the true deity of Jesus for the
church. That is why this truth is so clearly emphasized
in the Nicene Creed. They have gone on saying it to this
very hour, and again, it is not only people outside the
church, who are spiritually ignorant and uninformed,
but often it is the leaders within the organized church
of today who say, "Jesus is not true God with the Father
and with the Holy Spirit."

Jesus said, "The Son of Man is come to seek and to
save that which is lost." Jesus said, "I am your Savior."

His enemies said, "You are not our Savior. You are a liar. You are a fraud." They said it then. They said it in the days of Paul, very soon after our Lord's ascent on high. They have continued to say it down to this very hour. All through the centuries men have rejected Jesus. They have not wanted the kind of a religion in which you had to bend your knee at the foot of the cross, and as a humble, penitent sinner embrace Jesus and say, "You are my Savior. You died for me. I trust in the blood which you shed on my behalf." They have torn down the altar of Christ. They have either set up no altar at all, as is true of great masses of people in Russia and as is true of great masses of people in the United States of America, or they have set up altars of another kind at which they have tried by their own devices and means to work out the demands of God. But Jesus they have rejected.

Jesus said in His day, "If you want to be happy, if you want a world of peace, then let each man love his neighbor as himself. Do unto others as you would have them do unto you. This," He said, "is what the Law of Love requires. This is the way to a happy adjustment of all human relationships." Men said then, and men say today, "That is not true. It is a lie." Men have gone their own way. They still are going their own way. They say, "It is not by love, it is not by kindness, but it is by the hellish power of an atomic bomb that you make men live at peace with you." And so they reject Jesus and will have nothing to do with Him.

Jesus said, "What God hath joined together let not man put asunder. Respect the holy bond that ties you to your wife or to your husband. It is only when you look upon this as a holy estate, when you see each other as a precious gift of God, when you live with one another from the day of marriage until 'death you do part' that you can have the happiness which God wants you to have." But men in great numbers have said, "We do not believe that. That is a lie. The only way you can be happy is to live out your own life. Accept no restraints. Do as you want to do, and don't let anybody impose bonds of enslavement upon you."

NO EVIDENCE

So as the years have gone by the attitude of men toward Jesus has not changed. When these people came with Jesus to Pilate, this Roman said, "What accusation bring ye against this man?" That was a fair question to ask. I do not think Pilate was very much concerned. He didn't greatly care whether justice prevailed or not. That was so not because the Romans did not have a good legal system. Oh, no. They had a rather highly developed legal system, and the idea of justice and fairness toward men was a tradition among them. As a good Roman governor, Pilate should have been very much concerned about doing that which was right and just. The laws of his country demanded that he should. But Pilate was not even a good Roman. Pilate was a crude politician, who, if tradition is right and credible, eventually died in exile by his own hand. Even the Roman government did not want anything to do with a scoundrel of his stripe. But if it was just as easy to be just as to be unjust, he would be just.—"What accusation bring ye against this man?" It was a simple, natural question for a judge to ask.—We still ask the question. If people reject Jesus, why do they reject Him?—Then, they were speechless. They had no intelligent and convincing answer to the question. There were no evidences to present.

It is still so to this very day. Nineteen hundred years of microscopic investigation and examination have been made of every detail of Christ's life, Christ's character, Christ's teaching; and still there are no accusations forthcoming against Him which men are able to support with evidence.

Each day there are I don't know how many millions of people in our country who, if they use the name of Jesus at all, use it only for profanity. Next to the name of God, the name of Jesus is the most common curse word in our country, perhaps in other lands, too. Why? What accusation bring ye against this Holy One that you so abuse Him?

The life of Jesus stands there above reproach. No one has ever pointed successfully to a flaw in our Lord's conduct. Sometimes men, trying to be facetious, have tried to make it appear as though they found some flaws in the character of Jesus, but whenever they did so, they only made fools of themselves. They revealed that they did not even understand the situation wherewith they were dealing. The character of Jesus is above just criticism. Even His enemies must admit that there never was a man like that. He is singular, exceptional in the history of the whole human family.

What is true of His life and of His character was true also of His public ministry. Would anyone dare to criticize the ministry of Jesus, when He taught so clearly, when He was so kind and sympathetic to all who needed His love, when He fed the hungry and pleaded for the widow and the orphaned, when He healed the sick, when He forgave the sinners who were crushed by the accusations of a guilty conscience? Who will criticize a ministry like that? No one has been able to surpass the glory of His teaching, not only inasmuch as it bears on Himself as the Way, the Truth, and the Life, without whom no man cometh to the Father, but also inasmuch as it bears on moral principles and ethical standards. Jesus was a humble Galilean. He was not

reared in the great universities even of that day. He
never proudly displayed a sheepskin in a frame hanging
on the walls of whatever His humble home may have
been; and yet, the moral thinking and teaching of Jesus
by far surpasses anything that ever came over the lips
of history's greatest philosophers, poets, writers of
drama, or moral and philosophical teachers. By uni-
versal consent He was the greatest, and yet, despite it
all, men reject what He taught. Why? Doesn't it
work? Have men discovered that when you apply the
teachings of Jesus to everyday life, it won't go? No,
the truth is, they have discovered the very opposite.

Use force in dealing with your fellowmen and you
have war, you have destruction, you have death, heartache, suffering, impoverishment. Use love and you en-
gender good will, you build foundations of peace, you
create conditions of prosperity in which men can happily, peaceably live out their lives. Indulge your lusts
and you fail. Each day finds you hungrier and more and
more dissatisfied than did the day before. Live a life
of decency, of high moral quality, and out of it come
joys and simple satisfactions which money cannot buy
and which cannot be gained in any other way. The
truth is that humanity has had a small measure of happiness, which has marked the degree to which it has
tried to walk in the foot-steps of Jesus, and humanity
has had an abundance of heartache and woe, misery and
suffering, which has marked the degree to which it has
rejected, condemned, accused, and hated Jesus.

So tonight once again, in the face of all that we can
observe in the world of our day, as our Savior stands
before us and masses of people hate and reject Him, we
must once again say as Pilate once did, "What accusation bring ye against this man?" None! Because there
is none to bring. Anything men might say against Him

would be a lie, as was the case of the false witnesses who appeared before the Sanhedrin. And yet despite His innocence He had to suffer and die.

THE INNOCENT SUFFERS FOR THE GUILTY

This is the significant thing. The Christ of our salvation, who was hated and rejected by men, eventually nailed to a cross, is the innocent Christ, and because He is the innocent Christ, that is why your heart can be freed from all of its heaviness. Had He not been the innocent Christ we would have no message for you. There would be no hope for your soul. But because He was the innocent Christ, He could stand in your stead and suffer on your behalf, the Just for the unjust, to bring you to God. "He hath born our griefs and carried our sorrows." "He hath borne our sins in His own body on the tree that we might be made the righteousness of God in Him." That is the blessed story of Christ. That is what the suffering of the innocent Jesus means. You should have a personal peace because you know that the Holy Son of God became man and in perfect innocence He, who had no knowledge of sin by reason of personal experience, bore sin, suffered the consequence of sin for you, so that you should be freed. That is what the Bible means when it says, "The blood of Jesus Christ, God's Son, cleanseth us from all sin." If I have a debt at the bank and you generously pay it, it is paid. If I believe you have paid it, my mind is at ease. I have no further worry about that debt. If I do not believe it, the burden of the worry is still with me. To me there has come no relief despite your love and kindness. Jesus the Innocent One, has put Himself into your place. He has borne the suffering you should have borne because of your transgressions. It is all paid for. All has been made right with God. Believe it. If you believe it, then you are happy. Then you can look God in the eye, as it were. You need never cast your eyes down in shame and hope that God does not find you out. You can be happy because you know the whole burden has been taken from you. But if you do not believe it, then of course for you it is as though Jesus had never come. The benefits of His suffering and dying will bring no peace to your heart because you refuse it. Accept it.

I do not think you would be here this evening, if you were not conscious of your sins. The other day a young person said to me, "There was a time when I could do anything I wanted to. It didn't bother me, because I was not aware that it was wrong. But now, since I know that it is wrong, I do not know what to do about it." I am sure you are here because sin worries you. It bothers you to know that you do not do what is right. This is what you should do about it: Trust in this innocent Jesus who suffered and died even though men could bring no accusations against Him.

INFINITE LOVE

If you put your faith in Him, then it must occur to you, as the Bible very clearly teaches, that this Jesus has an infinite love for you. If He loved you enough to suffer and to die for you, then that love must also apply to other interests in your life. He cannot die for you and then forget about you. If He died for you, then He has an infinite stake in you. Then He has shed His blood for you. Then you are a very precious being in His sight. He cannot forget you. That is what Jesus would like you to understand. When you watch this innocent Jesus suffer and die, that should be a measure of the love which is in His heart for you. Life poses many situations for which I do not have the answers, and for which you do not have the answers either. Many difficulties and problems arise in our lives and we ask ourselves: why is this? Why should this sorrow come to

me? Why should this cross come to my family? Why
should this individual who has worked so hard and been
so honest have all of his life's savings wiped away? And
so on and so on. Who will begin to ennumerate all of
the problems of life that come? And yet, through all
of these heavy, dark clouds which hover over us, and
which surround us, and through which we cannot look
with our own eyes, there shines a ray of light that never
fails, a ray of light which comes from this loving Christ.
When you do not have any other answer, then you still
have this one answer: "Be quiet now. Don't get yourself all exercised. Don't wear yourself out with a lot
of needless worry. Trust in Jesus. He loves you. His
love will never fail you. He died for you. Don't forget
that. Trust in Him."

BE GRATEFUL

So, you see, this question which Pilate once asked,
"What accusation bring ye against this man?" points a
truth which has meaning for every day of our lives.
You cannot even listen to that question and think about
it, without having it grip you, without having it say to
you, "What are you going to do about it?" If the Innocent Christ has won salvation for me, if the Innocent
Jesus, by His suffering, has given me an unfailing assurance that in every situation of life He is right at my
side, by day and by night, in good days and in evil, well,
then, what am I going to do about it? Doesn't it call for
anything? Oh, certainly, I cannot let someone be kind
to me and shower me with His grace and goodness and
love, and never say 'thank you.' What kind of a wretch
would I be? What sort of a heart would be within my
breast, if it sensed no gratitude toward those who are
good to me? How then can I take this gift, the suffering of the Innocent Son of God for me, the guilty sinner,
without trying day by day in life to express my thanks

to Him? A man cannot accept the love of his wife without feeling a sense of gratitude. No woman can accept the love, the care, and the generous treatment of her husband without feeling a sense of gratitude toward him. No thoughtful children can take all that their parents give them without feeling that they owe them something. They would like to say 'thank you.' They would like somehow by their behavior to make them happy and to express their gratitude. Well, just so, my friends, you and I cannot watch this Innocent Jesus suffer the torments of hell without resolving that as God gives us strength we are going to show Him that we are grateful. And so, day by day, we find each hour a new challenge as well as a new opportunity. No matter what you do, whether you are making a breakfast for daddy and the children, whether you are answering the 'phone, whether you are having a patient in the dental chair, or whether you are standing over a patient at the operating table, always there is going through your heart and mind this one great, important, driving thought, "I must show my Lord that I appreciate what He has done for me. How can I do it? I want Him to know that I am grateful."

And my friends, right there lies the secret of a happy, blessed life. There also lies the one and only approach to the real lifting of human society. So when Pilate asked this question, "What accusation bring ye against this man?" he pointed at the Innocent Jesus who has such infinite meaning for us.

THE ROYAL CHRIST

"Jesus answered, 'My kingdom is not of this world: if My kingdom were of this world, then would My servants fight, that I should not be delivered to the Jews: but now is My kingdom not from hence."—John 18: 36.

✦ ✦ ✦

A S GOD grants grace, we want to focus our attention in this hour on "The Royal Christ." Our topic is based on the word of Jesus which He spoke to Pilate as recorded by John. We read, "Jesus answered, 'My kingdom is not of this world.'"

JESUS THOUGHT OF AS EARTHLY KING

Ever since Jesus came into this world people have tried to make of Him an earthly king. They have conceived of Him as another Caesar Augustus, or King Herod, or Joseph Stalin, or King George VI, or Harry Truman. Sometimes they have thought of Him as a king who had a little earthly kingdom and who was greatly to be feared. Sometimes they have thought of Him as a king with a little earthly kingdom who was greatly to be desired.

King Herod was one of those who thought of Him as a rival for his throne. He was so afraid that Jesus was going to be the kind of a king he was, that Jesus was going to sit in his place, that he gave command to have all the little children in and about Bethlehem to be killed. He wanted to make sure that Jesus would never take his place.

The enemies who took Jesus captive in the Garden of Gethsemane and who brought Him to Pilate accused Him of being a revolutionary, a man who was trying to subvert the rule of the Emperor and make Himself a rival ruler. When Pilate heard this, he pricked up his ears. This was something in which he was greatly interested. If Jesus really was a man who wanted to sit in the place of the Emperor, well, then it was time that he should give the matter thought.

Down to very recent times, to our own very day, there have been those who have thought of Jesus as a king whom they had to fear, one who wanted to take their place and push them out of their position of power and of government. Hitler thought of Jesus that way. He conceived of Jesus as his rival. That was why he was so bitter against Christianity. Lenin and Stalin have thought of Jesus in that way. That is why they have left no stone unturned in their effort to stamp out Christianity in their great country.

Then again, there have been those who have conceived of Jesus as a little earthly king with a little earthly government over which He would rule, but who was a desirable king. That was the attitude of the people whom Jesus had fed by miracle. Oh, they thought that would be wonderful, if they could have their own little country and then have Jesus as their king, who, without any effort on their part, would keep them well fed and nourished. That would be glorious.

This idea, too, has persisted. We still have people in this world who would like to put Jesus into the place of Chiang-kai-Chek or into the White House. They would like to give Jesus a very efficient police force and then let Him dictate on the basis of the Sermon on the Mount what the principles should be by which life should be lived. The police force would then take action whenever anyone violated the principles of this Sermon on the Mount. You see, to our very day human beings still have the idea that Jesus really is a rival of the earthly ruler. Some think He would be a ruler to be feared and some think He would be a ruler greatly to be desired, but all this while Jesus has had no such idea about Himself.

JESUS A DIFFERENT KIND OF KING

He said to Pilate, "My kingdom is not of this world." You notice, He did not disclaim royalty. Jesus did not say, "Please do not call me king; I am not a king." Oh, no, He accepted the idea that He was a king. "Thou sayest it, I am a king," only not the kind of a king Pilate and His enemies thought Him to be, the kind Herod thought He was going to be, or the kind the people who were hungry would like to have had Him be. No, He came to establish a different sort of a kingdom. He was a king who came from God, from heaven, to build among men the kingdom of heaven. He did not come to take the place of Harry Truman or of King George VI or of Joseph Stalin. They do not need to be worried about Him. He doesn't want their job. He came to do something altogether different in this world. Jesus saw human beings in all of their heartaches, in their misery, their worry, their sorrow. It was His commiseration for men which drew Him down from the heavens. He did not come to put Himself upon the throne and pass laws and collect taxes, raise armies, and wage wars. No, He came to bring something into human hearts they did not have. Jesus saw all of these human beings going around in circles not knowing where to find real peace and happiness.

When He looks down on human beings today, He discovers that what He has to offer them is just as important and necessary now as it was nineteen hundred years ago. To this very day human beings are going around in circles. We often speak of people being on a merry-go-round. Well, what do we mean? We mean that they are going round and round and never getting anywhere. There is no meaning to their lives. There is no purpose in their lives. They do not know where to start and whither to go. They know not where they are.

All of life is for them a matter of confusion and per-
plexity. So they try frantically to fill in the vacuum in
their lives. Only yesterday a young woman said to me,
"Before I found out about Jesus there was no meaning
in my life. I was irritable. I was cross. I was unkind
to my family. I deliberately did things that were wrong.
I was very unhappy. I was looking for something and I
did not know what I was looking for. I did not know
until I found Christ." That is true of only God would
know how many people. That explains this merry-go-
round existence to which they are devoting themselves.
Some think they are going to fill the vacuum of their
hearts by the pursuit of money. Others think that
amusements and pleasures will fill in and satisfy that
inner hunger, that longing for something, whatever it
may be. So they give themselves to the pursuit of pleasure. They are always on the go. They are always
looking for something new to keep them entertained and
occupied, hoping that someday they will land something
that will satisfy. Some seek their satisfactions in the
pleasures of sex, others in the attainment of fame, but
they are always on the go. By day and by night they
are looking for something until they get themselves
fairly exhausted. Jesus sees all of this and His heart
bleeds for these poor, unhappy, miserable humans. He
loves them all.

So Jesus let Himself be called from the heavens by
this pitiful situation of the human family, and He went
about and took from the souls of the humans all of their
transgressions. He determined to put away that whole
burden of sin. He was going to pay for it all. There
should be no further guilt. And then He would offer to
each human being this heavenly peace. He would rap
at the door of every heart. He would plead with every
sinner, "Come, let me in. Let me bring to you the peace

of God.   Let me fill your soul with quiet, with happiness, with this peace of heaven which surpasses all understanding."—That was the kingdom which Jesus came to establish on earth, not a kingdom of this world, not one in which people use force and guns and wage wars. He had no intention of being a rival of Herod or Caesar or George VI or Stalin, no, "My kingdom is not of this world."   "My kingdom is a kingdom of life, of truth, of grace, of peace," said Jesus.

BLESSINGS OF MEMBERSHIP IN CHRIST'S KINGDOM

If you are a member of that kingdom, be grateful. Sometimes it would appear as though individuals who are members of this kingdom never familiarize themselves with the joys and the blessings thereof.   They do not really become intimately acquainted with their kingdom.   They are like a great many people who live in these United States of America.   Here we have a vast country with every conceivable kind of scenery, with majestic mountains and broad, fertile valleys, streams and forests, enchanting lakes, every kind of climate, every form of scenery, and yet they are never looking around in the United States.   They are always looking forward to the day when they can take a trip to some foreign country to see some beautiful scenery.   They remind one of the people who think that everything would be ideal in our country, if only we could have the conditions which exist in Russia.   They have never yet found out what democracy really stands for, and they have no conception of what Russia is like.   Well, so it is with a great many Christians.   They have opened a little crack in their hearts and allowed Jesus to come in, but they have not become more closely acquainted with Jesus.   They have not looked around in His kingdom to see what blessings, what joys, what hope, what happiness such membership provides.   If Jesus has come to you and brought to you the assurance of His love and His forgiveness, then try, as God grants grace, by the enlightening influence of His Holy Spirit to become ever more intimately acquainted with this king and with the blessings of His kingdom so that you can revel in these gifts of divine mercy and grace.

This king who came from heaven, not to be a rival of earthly rulers, but to bring peace into human hearts and to establish in this world of strife and turbulence an oasis of quiet and of peace, would also have us understand that He has yet another kingdom. This kingdom of peace and quiet, which we have here in this world of turmoil and of noise, is only the ante-room, as it were, to that other kingdom. Here in this kingdom, even though Jesus comes and brings us peace, we still do find ourselves surrounded by all of the forces of evil which are in this world. Even our own heart still revolts against the rule of Christ. So we are adversely affected by many things.

Death, sickness, poverty, catastrophic experiences such as floods, fires, volcanic eruptions and all that sort of thing affect us. No matter how fine our Christianity, we still have not attained to perfect, complete, unceasing joy and happiness. One day we have tears of joy, the next day tears of sadness. One moment we laugh, the next we weep. One moment we see everything clearly, the next moment we are troubled and perplexed, and so it is. So long as we are in this world the grace of our Lord, membership in His kingdom of love and of mercy gives us strength, enables us to come through all of these trials. But nevertheless the struggle is still there. But one day the struggle shall end in complete and abiding victory. Our Lord is the Lord of glory. We shall be with Him "where there is fulness of joy and where there are pleasures forevermore." He, indeed, is a King. He is the royal Christ, the Christ who came to the crown of glory by way of the cross. This is the Christ who has redeemed all men and won for all men an eternal inheritance. This is the Christ who now invites you to come to Him, to worship Him as your Lord and King, and to look forward to the day when you shall surround His throne throughout eternity with all the angels and the saints of God to sing the praises of His Holy Name without being disturbed by heartaches and by fears. There all tears will be wiped away, all wounds healed, all strife over. Indeed, He is the royal Christ.

May it please our heavenly Father by His Holy Spirit to make us all the loyal subjects of this king so that we may here be guided by His Word of life and there be enriched with the treasures purchased by His blood. May God help us to kneel before Him and to hail Him as our blessed Lord, the Lord of lords and the King of kings.

THE MOCKED CHRIST

"Then came Jesus forth, wearing the crown of thorns, and the purple robe. And Pilate saith unto them, 'Behold the man!' "—John 19: 5.

THE text for our message this evening is taken from the Gospel according to St. John chapter 19, verse 5, where we are told, "Then came Jesus forth wearing the crown of thorns and the purple robe."

Last week we meditated on "The Royal Christ." Pilate, his servants, his military aides saw nothing royal in Christ. His outward appearance was humble and lowly and they could not imagine that any one such as He could be a king. He had no money. There were no outward manifestations of grandeur. He had no royal court. There was no clanging of swords and there was no military entourage, only a lowly person known as Jesus of Nazareth.

UNRECOGNIZED GREATNESS

Since that day many have failed to see greatness and royalty where they should have found it. We humans are so prone to look at everything from the outside, to judge things by their outward appearance. We have an idea that wherever there is apparent wealth or power or splendor there must also be something that is of real value. But when we see one who is lowly and humble, it doesn't occur to us that right there we might be in the presence of true greatness. We so easily forget that the world's manifestations, which are so impressive, might be used to hide that which is evil and damnable, whereas lowliness and humility may be the garments of genuine greatness.

We can see this from man's attitude toward Jesus. Men have not understood. How could He be great, a Jesus who was born of a maid; who came from Galilee;

140

who as a child had to flee to a foreign country to escape
His foes; who as a boy grew up in the home of an ordinary craftsman; who did not enjoy the advantages of
association with the great of this world; who never
knew what it meant to have a substantial bank account;
who during the days of His public ministry commonly
associated with the humblest of individuals, even with
those who were the outcasts of the supposedly higher
levels of society? No. He could not possibly be great.
Even to this day there are many who fail to see Jesus
as a royal Christ.

JESUS MOCKED

Pilate, his servants, his soldiers thought it an occasion for special sport when Jesus was on trial. So here
was one who dreamed that he was a king! Well, if He
thought He was a king then why not treat Him as a
king? At least, one could have some fun out of the
situation. So they took Him away. They abused Him.
They threw some purple robes about Him, for royalty
wore purple garb. Then they pressed a crown of thorns
upon His brow. Now He was a king! We can imagine
the scornful laughter, the bitter, contemptible, blasphemous mockery which all of this occasioned. How these
men must have carried on in the presence of the Son of
God as they tauntingly clothed Him like a king!

If men have at all times been tempted to underrate
the significance of Jesus because of His outward appearance of lowliness, they have, like Pilate and his associates, also at all times found a great deal of joy in making fun of Jesus, of treating with mockery and scorn the
story of Christ and His redeeming love. "How ridicu-
lous," they say, "that Jesus should have been born of
a virgin. Don't we know that there are other characters
in history who are alleged to have had a virgin birth?
Are we so stupid as not to realize that this is one of

those myths which grew up around Him?" So the whole story of Christ's virgin birth is treated with contempt. They say, "Are we to be so stupid as to believe that Jesus actually performed miracles? Don't you realize yet that Jesus knew how to make mind function over matter, that He was able to make things look like miracles?" Thus many of those things which are told us about Jesus are treated with laughter and with scorn even in this day. The idea that Jesus should have died to pay for the sins of men, that He should have shed His blood as the Son of God who became a human and took upon Himself the total human guilt, who would believe anything so absurd? How can a bloody theology of this nature be the theology of God? This is something which has been concocted by the priests of bygone generations and which is still being purveyed by those who make their living out of the ministry today. And so Jesus has suffered through the centuries. When Paul told the audience on Mount Areopagus about the resurrected Christ they laughed. "Nobody ever arose from the dead, neither did Jesus." And so through the centuries, year after year and century upon century, men have toyed with the teachings of Jesus. Some have scornfully despised what Jesus has done in His infinite love to work out the salvation of men's souls.

FOR YOU

Despite all this mockery and all this scorn, our text says, "Then came Jesus forth wearing the crown of thorns and the purple robe." There is more in those few words than I am able to tell you, I am sure, but let me point out only a few things which we do not want to miss. We read, "Then came Jesus forth wearing the crown of thorns and the purple robe." Who was this Jesus? This Jesus was you. He was not there for His own benefit. He was there in your place. When you see Him despised and crowned with thorns, then you see what happens to us when we are the servants of sin. This is what sin does. This is not what sin promises to do. This is what sin always does.

When you listen to the blandishments and to the promises of sin you will discover that it is always holding forth something that will be lovely and fine and satisfying. It was so in Paradise. "Should God have said that you should not eat of that tree? Why that cannot be. Certainly it cannot harm you to eat of that tree. God knows that you will be like unto Him if you will eat of that tree." Such is the promise of sin. Whenever you are tempted to do something wrong there always goes with the temptation a promise that this time something which is wrong is going to turn out well. This one time, if never before in all the history of mankind, this one time something wrong is going to bring you a really desirable reward. This one time sin is going to make you happy. It may never have made anybody else happy. It may never again in all history make anyone happy, but if you will only do this one wrong thing it will make you happy. Oh, how many souls are languishing in hell because they listened to that kind of a promise! Who will begin to tell how many people there are up and down this country tonight who are clothed in the mockery of purple and who have pressed upon themselves a crown of thorns, who are, in other words, humiliated, grieved and tortured because they listened to the voice of sin?

Jesus was a perfect symbol of what happens to the sinner when he lets himself be misled. Sin never puts a golden crown upon anyone's head, a crown encrusted with beautiful jewels. Sin never clothes anyone with a truly royal purple robe. Oh, no, sin always pays out with thorns and rags, with scorn and shame.

If only we could learn this lesson, how much pain and suffering we could spare ourselves, and how many worries we could keep from the hearts and minds of our dear ones! If every husband and every woman here tonight could learn this lesson there would be so many happier days and years ahead for many a human. If all of you men and women, who are out in the world of business, could learn this lesson you could spare yourselves so much disappointment. Oh, if our sons and daughters could learn this lesson, how much greater would be the joy of fatherhood and motherhood, and how much less the worry and care about one's growing children.

JESUS REVEALS GREATNESS OF OUR SINS

"Jesus went forth wearing a crown of thorns and the purple robe," a symbol of the sinner and of what happens to him in the service of sin. But mark well, Jesus did go forth. And He went forth garbed in this way. This was the Son of God. This was not an ordinary man. This was not some itinerant jester whom they picked up and made the butt of their sport for a little while. No, this was the Son of God who had left the eternal mansions to take up His abode with men here below. Here was divine majesty being subjected to unspeakable indignities. Why did Jesus endure all this? Only because He came to pay for your sins. There was the Son of God standing in your place, wearing these rags and this crown for you. That gives you an idea of what your sins really amount to.

It is so difficult for us humans to see and understand clearly the full extent of our spiritual need. Theoretically almost anyone will subscribe to the idea of sin, but chiefly as a theory, as something in the abstract. There may be such a thing as sin, we admit, but when you actually get down to what is sin and where is it to be found, you must look for it in other people, not in me, not in you, always in somebody else. Well, are we perfect? Oh, no, we are not perfect, but, as we suppose, the wrongs we do are not very important. Aren't they? Do you think Jesus would have come forth wearing the crown of thorns and purple rags, do you think the Son of God would have allowed Himself to be thus abused and humiliated, had it not been made necessary by the seriousness of our sins? Would you really want to know how bad your sins are, then look at Christ, the mocked, the thorn-crowned Christ.

When Jesus came forth, caricatured in this way, Pilate called to His accusers and said, "Behold the Man!" It was a pitiful spectacle, indeed. Yet, this was what Jesus had to endure in order to atone for your sins. If your sins were as insignificant as you would like to think, then there would have been no need for such suffering on the part of Jesus. If you want to get a true picture of the sin that is in your soul, then you must have a good long look at Jesus as He comes forth wearing the crown of thorns and the purple robe.

CHRIST'S SHAME OUR COMFORT

But don't despair. It is true, the clearer we get to see our sins, the more God enables us to recognize the true state of our souls, the lower our heads will hang with shame. But if we continue to look at Jesus then we will also learn from this pitiful picture how infinite is His love for us.

Think of it! The Son of God was ready thus to endure for you. Many situations arise in our lives because of which we wonder whether God loves us. We often ask ourselves the question, why does God let this happen to me? Why doesn't God give such and such things to me when He gives them to others? Why is it that I am limited in this way or in that way? We are always tempted to quarrel with God and to behave ourselves as though God did not love us. Well, if ever any doubt arises in your heart as to whether God loves you, then look at this mocked and humiliated Christ.

When you see Jesus suffer for you in this way, then you should know, first of all, that He suffered to atone for all of your sins, no matter how great and numerous they may have been. He bore infinite suffering. There is no sin for which He did not atone. The picture of the thorn-crowned Christ should also tell you that God's love will never fail you in any situation of life. God will never walk out on you. Jesus, your best Friend and your truest Physician, will never forsake you. Others may have no answer to your problems, but there is One to whom you can speak with complete assurance, and One upon whose unfailing love you can always rely. Holy Writ assures you that you will never be disappointed or put to shame because of your trust in Christ. If you want the measure of His love, then look at Him as He stands there, abused, disgraced, humiliated for your sake.

OUR LORD'S SUFFERING CALLS FOR GRATITUDE

When Pilate said to the enemies of Jesus, "Behold the man!" he no doubt thought that he would soften their hearts a bit so that they would conceivably be ready to grant some mercy, but the effect was the very opposite. When Pilate appealed to the hearts of Christ's accusers, they had only one answer. They said, "Crucify Him, crucify Him." They were not touched. Their sympathies were not aroused. They hated Jesus.

While it is true that there have always been those who have rewarded the love of Jesus with bitterness and with unrelenting hatred, you and I ought learn from the love which He has shown us to love Him. How is it possible for any one of us to picture ourselves as standing there, garbed as He was, without feeling a deep debt of gratitude to the One who so suffered on our behalf? The very picture of Jesus crowned with thorns and cloaked in a purple robe should be to us an invitation to pour out our lives in love to God and to our fellowmen. If we really want an example as to what we should be ready to do by way of expressing our love and of showing that the spirit of Christ is in our hearts, then the purple robe and the crown of thorns ought serve us well. Real love demands more than nice words. It is not enough that we merely subscribe to the Golden Rule. But how far are we really ready to go to show our love? What do we say when something needs to be done for the cause of Christ and humanity? Don't we often say, "Why should I do that? Why should I be the fool? Why should I pay the price? Why should I wear that robe of purple rags and pierce my scalp with a crown of thorns? Not I. Let somebody else do that." But that wasn't the way Jesus handled the situation. "Then came Jesus forth, wearing the crown of thorns and the purple robe." This is the picture by which you and I should be guided as we make our journey through this world. So, the mocked Christ who was so shamefully abused, like the royal Christ and the innocent Christ, again brings to our hearts rich comfort and mighty inspiration.

May the Spirit of God use these blessed truths for our good here in time and hereafter in eternity.

THE CROSS-BEARING CHRIST

"And He bearing His cross went forth into a place called the place of a skull, which is called in the Hebrew Golgotha."—John 19: 17.

✓ ✓ ✓

I HOPE that by the mercies of God this will be an hour of spiritual benefit to each of you as we reflect on the picture of "The Cross-Bearing Christ." Our thoughts are based on the sacred record given by John, chapter 19, verse 17, where he records, "And He (that is to say, Jesus) bearing His cross went forth into a place called the place of the skull, which is called in the Hebrew, Golgotha."

JUSTICE TAKES A HOLIDAY

Jesus had been placed before Pilate to be tried on the charges which His enemies brought against Him. His accusers were not able to establish any guilt, but the trial had come to no good end. If we ask, why was it that Jesus had to bear His cross and go forth on the Way of Sorrows, the only answer is, because justice failed Him. Justice took a holiday. The voice of sin and injustice spoke up. Though He has innocent, yet He was condemned and sent forth under the burden of the cross.

This is not the only time in history, unfortunately, that injustice has prevailed. If you and I make our way through the pages of history, we can say that injustice shrieks at us from almost every page. You can turn back to the earliest days of the human family, come on down through the ages, and you will find "injustice," "injustice" stamped on every page of every age.

When the Children of Israel were in Egypt they were subjected to the particular injustices of the Egyptian Pharaoh. When the prophets preached and brought the message of God, they had to cry out again and again against the injustices which were perpetrated by the powerful and by the rich upon the poor, the widows, the orphans. When Jesus stood trial He suffered injustice.

We who live in this supposedly enlightened twentieth century know just as much about injustice as did all the generations that went before. We have a great body of law. It is designed and intended to serve the ends of justice, but we know that men are often corrupt, that graft plays a large part in the supposed administration of justice. Officials holding public office often are bribed. Police frequently are put under orders. The worst criminals sometimes are shielded and protected. Gambling, drunkenness, prostitution, all carry on unabashed with the benefit of illegal protection. The meanwhile the peave-loving, tax-paying, and law-abiding are denied the benefits and the protection which should be accorded them by these very officers of the law. We have lived to see a day when the injustices perpetrated by the powerful and by the rich upon the poor are not so common in our own land. We have lived to see the day in which that situation has been turned around in quite an unexpected manner. Today it is not uncommon to see those who are supposed to be powerful and who are supposed to be rich subjected to the injustices forced upon them by the unthinking, the greedy, and the selfish who manipulate those who constitute the working classes.

Look where you will, and you get a picture of injustice. Leave public life, industrial life, and step into the privacy of this home and that home. Here you find a poor wife and mother who has worked all day trying earnestly, conscientiously to fulfill her duties, to care for her home and children, to provide for her husband only to find that when he comes home, he has no heart for his dear ones. He taunts them and subjects them to mental cruelty, perhaps even to physical abuse. Or it may be the other way around. A man tries honestly to do his best to provide for his family. Yet, when he comes home instead of finding a haven of peace, a place of refuge where he can turn away from all the bitter cruelties of life, he is met by one who treats him abusively, who nags him, who gives him no rest of mind nor peace of heart, who is constantly disagreeable, never pleased with the things that are done for her. And so the poor man wears out his life. What should he do? Day after day he finds himself subjected to these injustices.

I do not think that the most eloquent could give an adequate description of the suffering that has come into human life because of injustices perpetrated by one human upon another or by one organized group upon another group of human beings. We find it in international relationships. We find it wherever we look. Tonight as we look upon the figure of the cross-bearing Jesus, we see Him the victim of injustice.

JESUS ENDURED INJUSTICE FOR YOU

You say, "Why should Jesus suffer injustice?" Well, my friends, you are looking at the Lamb of God that came to take away not only some sins, not only certain sins, but the sins of the world. Among these, the sin of *injustice* plays a prominent part. Jesus came to be the Redeemer also of us humans who so often make ourselves guilty of unjust acts in relationship to one another.

Our text says, "And He, bearing His cross, went forth." I do not know how much that cross weighed. It was made of wood. I would not know what kind of wood. But howsoever heavy or light it may have been, it should not have been laid on Christ. He had had nothing to eat, nothing to drink. He had had no rest. He had been subjected to the most violent kind of abuse. He had lost blood. He had suffered the anguish of hell in Gethesemane. This cross, whatever it weighed, was, humanly speaking, too heavy for Him. And yet it was not the physical weight which pressed down most, for this cross really was a symbol. It was not what that piece of wood weighed in and by itself that mattered chiefly, but it was rather what that piece of wood represented, for this cross was a symbol of all the burden that rested upon the whole human family. Run through the total catalog of human wrong-doing, whether you think of the lying, the dishonesties of the young; whether you think of the greed, the vanity, the envy, the jealousy, the hatred, the bitterness of those who have come into more mature years; or whether you think of the selfishness, the miserliness, the self-righteousness of those who have attained to old age; whether you think of crimes of violence or the more refined forms of wrong-doing which are more subtle and not so easily detected by those of untrained moral sensibilities; all of these things are represented by that cross, and they were all lying on Jesus. "And He, bearing His cross, went forth." My friends, that is a wonderful statement.

That is a statement designed by the Spirit of God to bring comfort to your heart and to my heart. It doesn't make any difference who you are, where or when you may have fallen, what the particular burden may be that rests on your conscience, Jesus wants to have you see Him carry that sin away. Here you have a picture of infinite love. Would to God that this love might find its way into every human heart.

We so often speak now-a-days of the tensions of life. We are often told how physical illnesses, which result from these tensions, are multiplying. Every now and then we hear of some man who should have been in the prime of life but who fell over dead because his heart gave out or because he suffered a stroke. Well, life is

rugged these days, and I suppose it is difficult to hold
any kind of a responsible position in the world of business or in the professional world without having to give
a tremendous amount of energy to it. Those who have
the responsibility of leadership find themselves burdened
with cares brought on by the very uncertainties of our
time. And yet, when you analyze it all, you finally get
down to this one thing: that there is nothing which
makes men so tense, which keeps them in such a constant state of jitters and uneasiness, as does the sense
of guilt. Were men not burdened by a sense of guilt, their
hearts would be light and they could face life with much
finer confidence and with much greater courage. Whatever others may do, and howsoever they may insist upon
torturing and tormenting themselves, don't you make
that mistake. Let the Spirit of God open your eyes.
Have a look at this cross-bearing Jesus. See Him stum-
bling along under the burden of that cross. There go
your sins, all of them, and God wants you to be sure of
it. He wants you to have heavenly joy and peace in your
soul. He wants you to be able to look at every aspect
of life, at every problem which presents itself in your
profession, at your job, in your business, wherever it
may be, in your home—He wants you to see every one
of them in the light of this love which He has shown to
you. You are not to think of Him as an enemy. You
are not to think of Him as one who is waiting anxiously
for the moment when He can strike you. No, you
should think of Him as a Friend who is by your side.
He has taken your sins away. He loves you as His son,
as His daughter. He will hold your hand firmly and
lead you through whatever the problems and difficulties
of your earthly journey may be, be they of a temporal,
physical, be they of a spiritual, eternal nature. He is
there to help you. So open up your heart wide and let
the love of God, as shown you in Jesus Christ, come in,

take away the anxieties, the worries, and fill you with peace and with joy.

HOPE FOR MANKIND

This picture of the suffering Christ weighted down by the burden of the cross which represents the sum total of all human guilt should also give us hope for human society. We have not learned very much since the days of one of the earliest Old Testament prophets, the prophet Jonah. You may remember, God wanted to send Jonah to Nineveh. Nineveh was a Chicago in its day, a great city, and of course in it were all of the sins so common to great cities. The Ninevites were behaving themselves very badly. God wanted to send them a warning, so He told Jonah in effect, "You go and warn these people. Call them to repentance." Jonah said in his heart of hearts, "Not on your life. I will never go there. That is a waste of time. They will not listen to me anyhow." That is our approach to the problems of human society today. You have no difficulty finding an appreciable number of professed children of God, followers of Jesus Christ who would say, "What's the use? Men are bad. Why preach the Word of God to them? Why try that? They will not listen anyhow." When we say that, we are really not passing so much judgment on other people as we are revealing what is in our own hearts. We are very self-satisfied and self-righteous human beings. We have an idea that God can accomplish things with us, but that He cannot accomplish the same things with others. We have an idea that we are pretty good material for the Spirit of God to work on, but that our brothers and sisters in the human family, outside our circle, are not so good to work on. And when we pass that kind of judgment we do not pay ourselves a very good compliment. We reveal ourselves as self-righteous human beings who neither understand the real love of Jesus Christ who bore His cross, nor appreciate that this cross represented not only your sins or my sins but the sins of the whole human family. Jesus carried them all away. So, we should not take the attitude of Jonah. Our view of the human situation should not be a hopeless one. We should rather make our attack upon human society as we can, trusting and believing that by the power of God's Holy Spirit and the love that shines down from Calvary's cross one heart and another heart and another one can be changed, as our hearts have been changed, and that men in all walks of life with every hue and color of skin and out of all the varied races round the globe can be brought to the foot of that cross to accept the same common Redeemer and to dedicate themselves to the living of a life patterned after Him.

JESUS WENT ALL THE WAY

As we look upon this Cross-bearing Jesus we learn, He went forth not only a little way, but, "He went forth into a place called the place of the skull, which is called in the Hebrew, Golgotha." After Jesus had been condemned so unjustly, his judicial murderers still followed out at least the letter of the law, though they had violated the meaning and spirit of it completely. They wrote on a little tablet the reasons because of which He was going to be executed. This tablet they tied around His neck. This was intended as a last possible chance to rescue anyone who was going to be condemned. The idea was that some one who could vouch for his innocence might see him while he was on his way to the place where he was to be executed. So they went through this procedure also with Christ. Then they put the cross on Him and sent Him forth. He could still have turned around. He could still have abandoned the whole project. It was not too late. But He did not. He went all the way, step for step over that Way of Sorrow, on to the Mound of Skulls, which may have been so named either because of its shape or because it was the place of public execution, there finally to reach the end of His long trail of pain and suffering. What a blessed truth, my friends! Jesus had come to do a certain thing. He said, "The Son of Man is come to seek and to save that which is lost." Had He hesitated anywhere along the road, had He changed His plans, gone off on a detour, given up, then you and I would have no hope. But He did not. He went all the way, and this is what gives assurance to our hearts. If there were any question about it so that only a little doubt could come through a small rift here or there, the whole game would be lost. Our souls would be abandoned to despair. But there is no such deficiency. The program is complete. The job is done, perfectly done. Nothing has been left undone. You should be at peace. Nothing should disturb you in your mind any more. "What must I do? Does God love me? Have my sins been atoned for? Can I rely upon it that He will hear my prayers? Are these things true which He teaches in His Holy Word? Will it really come out that way?" No, such questions need no longer trouble us. There is no more room for doubt. The task is completed. Jesus went the whole way. Your heart will always be quiet and strong as you remember that, and your heart will always be uneasy, fretful, fearful, as you forget that. So keep your eye on this Christ, this cross-bearing, suffering Christ as He goes to Golgotha.

HOW FAR WILL YOU GO FOR CHRIST?

But, my friends, we cannot stop here. We must present at least one more thought before we have done. Jesus went all the way for you. Does that suggest anything to your mind? Does it arouse any feelings within your heart? Does it call you to any kind of action, or doesn't it? Have you long since taken your eyes off Him and started to drift in your thinking, or is your eye on this Christ who goes all the way for you? If your eye is on Him, then you must be formulating in your heart a resolve that you are going to go all the way for Him. That is the point. Why do people laugh at the church? Why does the world with a gesture of contempt and disdain dismiss the church as though it were of no account in the affairs of men? Why is it that men can go on in their thinking about human society and all their problems without turning to the church? Well, my friends, only because the people who profess to be followers of this Christ do not go all the way with Him. They start. They take a few feeble steps, and then they turn away and march with the world.

Now just where are you? How far have you been going with Christ in your life, in your devotion, in your dedication to Him, in the consecration of your life, your talents, your possessions, all that you have? How much of your love and of your interest really goes into the worship of this Christ? What part does your Christian faith have in your life? How often do you have the cross of Jesus before your eyes? How often do you think of that radiant love that streams from Calvary bringing peace and hope to you, as compared to the number of times that you think of the world and all that the world is offering you? Oh, how sad and tragic it would have been if Jesus would have gone only part of the way. Well, from His point of view, it is just as sad and tragic for us to go only a part of the way with Him. There is no room in the program of God for an anaemic, weak, half-hearted kind of Christianity. If religion means anything, it means everything. If Christ plays any part in our lives, He must be the One who is the Master of our souls. If we say, we love Jesus, then it must be more than a matter of words. It must be the giving of our hearts and of our lives. And so as we close this meditation I want to call your attention once more to this picture of the cross-bearing Jesus. John says, "And He, bearing His cross, went forth into a place called the place of the skull, which is called in the Hebrew, Golgotha."

May God help you and help me to drink in the meaning of that word. Amen.

THE SINNERS' CHRIST

"They crucified Him and two others with Him, on either side one, and Jesus in the midst."—John 19: 18.

✦　　✦　　✦

T HIS evening we find ourselves on the brow of Calvary looking at "The Sinners' Christ." Our text is taken from the Gospel according to St. John, chapter 19, verse 18 where we are told, "They crucified Him and two others with Him, on either side one, and Jesus in the midst."

THE EXECUTIONERS

As we look upon the Sinners' Christ from this vantage point we find Him in the hands of His executioners. These are the hangmen of Pilate. They were Roman soldiers. Even as in this year of our Lord soldiers still are taught how to kill, so were they taught how to kill in that distant day. Whether their hearts were touched or whether they were not, we do not know. Our text merely states, "They crucified Him." That was Pilate's command and so they carried it out. But this text does not tell the whole story. This is only a part of the Biblical evidence which bears on the crucifixion of Jesus. Perhaps we would wish that this were the whole story, but it isn't.

If we take into consideration the total evidence of the Scriptures, then we learn that it was not only they, but also we who crucified Him. The Scriptures are very plain on this point. They say, "He was wounded for our transgressions; He was bruised for our iniquities." They say, "He hath borne our sins in His own body on the tree." They say, "He was made a curse for us." This affects us rather deeply. We cannot lift our heads up proudly and publish to the universe, "We crucified

Jesus." It need but be whispered that we crucified Jesus and then we must hang our heads in shame. So the very first effect which our view of the Sinners' Christ must have upon our hearts is this, that it moves us to a sense of shame and true repentance.

We see Jesus nailed to the cross. The Sinners' Christ is crucified. We have come to know the cross as a symbol of beauty representing everything that is noble and fine. It is extremely difficult for us even to conceive of the idea that at one time in history the cross was the symbol of abysmal and absolute disgrace. And yet so it was. It would not have occurred to people nineteen hundred years ago to wear the cross as a piece of jewelry symbolizing love, sacrifice, and nobility. It would not have occurred to people to place upon their buildings of worship a cross. The cross was so hated and so despised by all the people of the Roman Empire that they refused not only to talk, but even to think, about it. The very word seemed to be a desecration upon the lips of a Roman. And yet it was to the cross Jesus was reduced. He could have been beheaded. He could have been burned at the stake. He could have been destroyed by wild beasts. There might have been various ways in which they could have executed Him. They could have given Him a cup of poison such as was given to Socrates. But no, they crucified Him.

That was in order, because Jesus was there on account of sin, and crucifixion showed forth the real character of sin. A few days ago a gentlemen said to me, "I have never heard so much about sin as I have heard here at Grace Church." He said, "It seems to me like a message of negative character. It is negativism and not positivism." I said, "Yes, it does sound like a negative message, but what would you think of a dentist who would put gold into your hollow tooth before he had cut out all that was decayed? What would you think of a doctor who would sew up an infected wound before he had drained it or taken out all of the infection?" One reason why our Christianity so often is cold and indifferent is because we do not have a proper appreciation of the character of sin. It is not until you see Jesus on the cross that you really understand what a desperately tragic and destructive force sin is in the life of man. Sin always leads down, down to the deepest depths of degradation, and finally it ends in death..

While thinking about this it brought to my mind the instance of a young man who had a very wonderful personality, and was gifted in many ways, who enjoyed the friendship, the respect and the admiration of a great many people. But then the sin of drunkenness got hold of him and he started to go down. He never stopped until he had gotten to where the prodigal son had gotten, where, at least figuratively speaking, he shared the husks with the swine. And then he died. I think of another young man who probably at this very hour is hanging over a bar, bleary eyed, wrecked in health, a young man who has lost all ambition in life, whose self respect is low, whose finer moral and spiritual sensibilities and understanding have been killed because he has given himself over to the sin of drunkenness. Sin always leads down, down to the deepest depths of hopelessness and despair, and finally it ends in death. "They crucified Him" because He was the sinners' Christ. He came "to seek and to save that which was lost." "He, the Just, who knew no sin, came to be made sin for us." That is why He was crucified.

IN THE MIDST OF SINNERS

We find the sinners' Christ where He wanted to be. "They crucified Him and two others with Him, on either side one." That was the appropriate company for Jesus

—sinners, bandits, murderers, one to the right and one to the left. He had come here to seek out the company of sinners. If He did not want the company of sinners He might have stayed in heaven. But that was not His program. His program was to come and to keep company with sinners, because He loved sinners. His heart went out to sinners. He wanted to place the arm of love around them to protect them, to save them, to rescue them from the consequences of their sins. Look at the ministry of Jesus. You always find Him in the company of sinners. If He is not talking to God about sinners and for sinners, then He is with sinners. He is with sinners in a barn when He comes into this world. He is in the very surroundings of sinners when the command goes forth that He should be assassinated in early infancy. He lives with sinners in the despised areas of Galilee, about which men said, "What good can come from Galilee?" When He began to gather His little band about Him, He did not seek out individuals who were publicly reputed to be saints and great religious leaders. No, He went out and got those who were crude and rough sinners: a tax collector, a hot-headed fisherman, sons of thunder—all men who were sinners. The people who didn't like Him, didn't like Him because He was the sinners' Christ. They said, "He eats and drinks with sinners."

And, my friends, it is this very fact that He companied with sinners, that He hung on the cross with sinners, which is designed to bring so much comfort to us. Perhaps you wonder sometimes how close Jesus would come to you, how He would feel in your company. Well, you need not worry about how He would feel in your company. You have much more reason to wonder how you would feel in His company. Jesus has said, "Lo, I am with you always." He has said, "Where two or three are gathered together in My name, there am I in the midst of them." Here tonight is a whole audience of sinners, and Jesus is right with us. We gather in our homes and we are all sinners. We have our faults and our weaknesses. We are loveless. We are unkind. We are temperamental. We fail to control our tongues. Yet Jesus is there, if we want Him. He is there, because He is the sinners' Christ. He will never walk out on us or forsake us because we are sinners; no, it was because we are sinners that He came. He said, He did not come for those who are well, because people who are well do not need a physician. It is the people who are sick who need the doctor. He came to be the Physician for those who are sick in soul.

FOR SINNERS

But Jesus did not only hang on the cross in the midst of sinners. He also hung on that cross for sinners. These sinners who were crucified with Christ, whoever they may have been and whatever the catalog of their crimes and wrong-doings may have been, were a symbol, as it were, of the whole human family, and for them and for all that they might well have symbolized, Jesus hung on the cross. He is the Sinners' Christ.

Sometimes individuals do not appreciate Jesus. Whenever that is true, we can almost be certain that it is primarily because they do not understand their true spiritual needs. Whenever you have to argue with a man about going to church and about going to Holy Communion and about accepting the love and the mercy of God and all of the blessed assurance of forgiveness, then you can almost be certain, it is because that person has no clear understanding of his own spiritual needs. But when a person understands what evil there is in him, how his heart rebels against the will of his Maker, how he is always pulling away from the things that God would have him do, such a person finds the story of Jesus the sweetest story ever told. This story tells you that you are redeemed. It tells you that Jesus put Himself into your place and allowed the reward which you had merited by your sins to be paid out to Him. So when we look at the Sinners' Christ hanging on the cross it should bring reassurance and peace to our hearts and to our souls because it teaches us this blessed truth: all has been made well with God, because His only-begotten Son has atoned for our iniquities on the cross.

INFINITE LOVE FOR ALL

The fact that He gave Himself for us, allowed Himself to be nailed to that cross in our stead, is to us also a measure of His love. We often torture ourselves with all manner of worries and cares. We act as though we were in this world all by ourselves and as though in our loneliness we stood overagainst all the forces that oppose us. We forget that there is a Sinners' Christ who loves us, who loved us so much that He was crucified on our behalf. Oh, if only we could learn that truth. If only we could learn to use it, to apply it, to look at everything in life in the light of that truth. What a difference that would make. How glad our hearts would be. Then we could courageously and confidently face everything that might come up, because we would always know, the love of that Christ will not fail us. We might not be able to understand all of life. It might even seem all wrong to us. We might not be able to figure out how any good can come out of this or the other situation, and yet, if we know in our hearts, this love is there, then all is well.

Now, if you have looked at this sinners' Christ, if you have seen Him up there on the cross, and if you have seen the two characters that are on either side of Him, this will not only bring comfort to you but it will also give direction to your whole social thinking. You will never again be able to look at people like these two bandits with contempt. What were they? Murderers? Robbers? Whatever they were, we see Jesus in the midst of them. He was not ashamed of it. He did not refuse that place. He did not say, "Keep them away from ME. If you are going to crucify Me, I want to be crucified all alone. I do not want any such scum of the earth hanging around Me." Not a word of it. Right in the middle of them, one to the right and one to the left.

I wonder how we would behave ourselves if, let us say, a number of negroes were to come in here and take up their places in our pews. What would you do, if they sat down next to you? Get up? Go elsewhere? Or just how should we look at these poor Jews who have been persecuted in the lands where they have been living and who come to our country, vermin-ridden, diseased? Should we say, "We do not want anything to do with such unbathed individuals? Is that the way Jesus would have us look at them? Or what about all of these down-and-outers on lower Madison Street, the drunken men and the fallen women, the people in the last throes of moral and spiritual degeneration and decay? Well, if you and I want to learn how to think about such people and all of the other people whom we are inclined to treat from on top down, the Japanese, the Chinese, the Russians, and all the rest of them, then look at this: "They crucified Him and two others with Him, on either side one, and Jesus in the midst." That is where He wanted to be. He is the sinners' Christ—not only the Christ of sinners who wear white collars and who live in good homes, but the Christ of all sinners, from all walks of life, whoever they may be. And if you and I say, we are the disciples of Jesus, then there is our cue. It is not for us to talk as the world talks. It is not for us to accept our social views from people who are motivated by their own selfish interests. It is for us to learn how to look at our fellowmen through Him who was crucified in the midst of sinners.

DO YOU APPRECIATE WHAT JESUS DID FOR YOU?

If we look long enough at Jesus, the Sinners' Christ, and if we remember why He was nailed to the cross, then it must do something to our hearts. How can anybody look at Jesus and see Him bear what He bore without saying in the depths of his soul, "What can I do to express my appreciation to this Christ?"

Today I spent several hours with a gentleman whom we have had the privilege of instructing in the truths of God's Holy Word. It was very evident that this man had gotten a fine, clear conception of his own sins and of Christ as his Savior from sin. So I said to him, "You have expressed yourself in a very beautiful way about this. It seems to me that there ought be some evidence of this in your life. Your newly found faith ought make some difference in how you look at life and how you behave yourself." "Well," he said, "you know, I think it has." And then he went on to relate little experiences which he had with himself which astonished him. He told how he had gone to discuss a business venture with a certain man. When the conversation ended, the head of this venture said to him, "You know, you are a very unusual man." He did not mean that he was unusually intelligent. He did not mean that he was unusual because of the manner in which he was dressed. But he did mean that he was very unusual in his approach to life, in his attitude toward work, toward his fellowmen. That is how it must be. If you are not unusual in this respect then you had better look at your Christianity for a Christian must be unusual. If you are just a working man among workingmen, if you are just a businessman among businessmen, if your philosophy of life is like the philosophy of other businessmen who do the same kind of business you do, well, then, you have not stood long enough on Calvary. You have not seen this Christ correctly, for He is sending out this love to you so that there should be an outpouring of love from your heart into life overagainst your brothers and sisters. There is only one correct and satisfactory answer to Jesus and that answer is love.

So, you see, my friends, the Sinners' Christ has a great deal of meaning for us. This meaning applies to the life that now is and to the life that is to come. It tells us something about God's attitude to us and about our attitude toward God. May the Spirit of God help us learn well the meaning of the Sinners' Christ.

FOLLOW AFTER

"Not as though I had already attained, either were already perfect: but I follow after, if that I may apprehend that for which also I am apprehended of Christ Jesus."—Philippians 3: 12.

✓ ✓ ✓

THIS is a happy day because we once again have the privilege of receiving into the communicant membership of our congregation a number of men and women, boys and girls, who are ready to make a confession of their faith in the truths of God's inspired Scriptures. Even as this day is a happy day for us, so is it for many other Christian congregations in all parts of the globe, for in many other places services similar to this are being held. It does one's heart good to know that the Spirit of God continues to be active in human society. He still comes with the message of divine love to individual hearts and moves young and old, one by one, to accept Jesus as the personal Savior from sin. When we consider how much evil is abroad in the world, when we think how many individual hearts and souls are depressed by worry, by fear, and by the consciousness of guilt, then we cannot but thank God that He continues His work of mercy among men and goes on advancing His kingdom here on earth.

GROWTH IN QUALITY

While it is important that the kingdom should grow in quantity, in the numerical strength of its membership, it is also of importance that they who are the members of the kingdom should continue to grow in quality, in the quality of their faith, their spiritual understanding and their Christian life. This, I am very much afraid, we all are inclined to overlook and forget. I think I can truthfully say that my pastoral experience shows that too many of us are satisfied. We are satisfied with our spiritual attainments. We are satisfied with the quality of our conduct. We are satisfied with ourselves. I find too often that boys and girls who have been instructed for confirmation harbor the idea that now their religious training is complete. I find too seldomly that men and women who have been prepared for membership in the Church of Christ show an eagerness to continue their study of the divine Word. If that eagerness were present on the part of young and old, the size of our Bible Classes in Grace Church and the size of Bible Classes for young people of high school age and for adults in other Christian churches would be vastly greater than it is. This does not speak too well for the quality of our spiritual life. For if the quality of our spiritual life were better, we would not be so satisfied. We would show a greater eagerness to grow. How true that is, I can perhaps illustrate for you in no better way than by telling you how the apostle Paul thought about it with reference to his own state of soul. Paul said, "Not as though I had already attained, either were already perfect, but I follow after."

SPIRITUAL SHORT-COMINGS

It seems almost incredible that the apostle Paul should make such a statement. Few people in the history of the world have had the privilege of enjoying the rich full spiritual experiences which were his. Here was a man who had a heroic faith. Even in the darkest moments, when he did not know what was likely to happen next, he trusted God. This man had an understanding of Jesus and of the redeeming love of God in Christ which was perfectly amazing. This man had been moved by the Spirit of God to dedicate his life to the service of his Lord. He thought of himself as the slave of Jesus Christ. This man could honestly say in all humility that he had labored more than all the other apostles. This man had been even granted some special spiritual experiences in the form of remarkable visions. Yet, this was the man who said, "Not as though I had already attained, either were already perfect." Oh, Paul was so conscious of the deficiencies of his spiritual understanding. Here were the great truths of God and here was the little understanding of the apostle. He said, "Great is the mystery of God, God is made manifest in the flesh." He cried out, "Oh, the depth of the wisdom and the knowledge of God!" Overagainst this the little Paul was even smaller still.

Not only did he realize how little he knew, but he was also perpetually conscious of how little he did. He said, "What I would, I do not do and what I would not, I do. The spirit is willing, but the flesh is weak." So here was a real child of God and as his spiritual understanding grew, he recognized how many defects and deficiencies there were in him.

I could not help but think how analagous all of this is to life. When a little freshman starts out in high school and he has his first book introducing him to the sciences at hand, he very quickly comes to the conclusion that he knows all the answers. He now knows science. The reason why he thinks he knows all the answers is because he knows so little. On the other hand there is the great scientist, the one who enjoys a world-wide reputation, who is recognized as an authority in his field. When he speaks, he speaks with humility, for by reason of his great knowledge, he knows how little he knows of all that is to be known.

My friends, that is so important for us to understand. If we have anyone in our audience this morning who has the idea that he knows, will you not please accept that as the best assurance that your spiritual understanding is very deficient? You are like the youngster in high school who has read a few pages in a book of science and then thinks he knows all the answers. Listen to the apostle Paul, this great, experienced child of God, who had been given such special advantages and spiritual blessings. Hear what he has to say, "Not as though I had already attained, either were already perfect."

This applies not only to the boys and girls sitting before me, the members of our confirmation class, to the men and the women who will kneel at God's altar this morning, it applies to all of us. While thinking on this, I could not but recall again and again how as a boy I felt I knew the Catechism. Even when I was a student at the seminary it always affected me a bit queerly when the professors used to say that Luther called himself a student of the Catechism all his life, and that he asserted again and again that he had not quite learned that Catechism. It always seemed to me that Luther had been stretching a point when he made that statement. I think I now know a little bit whereof he was speaking. Each time God reveals another facet in the glorious jewel of divine truth and heavenly love, one becomes only the more conscious of how little one knows and how little one understands. We learn how determined we are to cut God, and the truths which He has revealed to us, down to our own size instead of allowing God to speak to us, to enlarge our spiritual understanding and to ennoble our lives and characters.

DETERMINED TO GROW IN KNOWLEDGE

Paul, who was conscious of the deficiencies in his spiritual life, did not accept that situation with complacency. He did not say, "I am still looking for a great many things but spiritual truth I already know." No, he said, "Not as though I had already attained, either

were already perfect, *but I follow after*." His spiritual
life to him was an adventure. It was something in
which progress and growth were to be marked each
passing day. Whenever Paul came to the end of another year, he wanted to feel that by the mercies of God
he had gone deeper into divine truth, he had come closer
to his God, he had grown stronger in his faith and clearer in his understanding. "I follow after."

And this, my friends, must be our motto in life, if
ours is to be a living Christianity, if our hearts are to
throb with spiritual life and vigor. When Paul said, "I
follow after" he was not making words. He expressed
a great truth. He grew in knowledge. When he was a
boy, he had learned of the law of Moses and of the Old
Testament prophecies. This was all he had known until
he had come into manhood. It was not until that memorable moment when he stood face to face with the
resurrected and the living Lord, who appeared to him
just before he reached the city of Damascus, that he
came to know Jesus as his personal Savior. He had indeed heard about Him. He had learned many things
about Him from his association with the Christians, but
he had never before known Him and believed in Him.
But after he had come to know Him, he spent time in
reflecting on this great and blessed truth that Jesus was
indeed the Son of God who had come into this world to
take the sins of all men upon Himself and to suffer and
die so as to work out the salvation of their souls. This
so fascinated Paul, this was so much in the front of his
mind that in his own thinking and in his own preaching
he professed to know nothing save Christ and Him crucified. That was the most marvelous of all truths. This
was something so great, it spoke so fully of the love and
the mercy of God, Paul could never sufficiently marvel
at the fact that Jesus, the Son of God, had become man

and given Himself on the cross as his Redeemer. So Paul grew from what he had learned in his childhood up to what he had come to know of Jesus when he preached the great sermons of the living Christ.

This is a way in which, beyond all others, you and I have reason to grow. We forget how prone we are to think that God is as we are and to evaluate the love of God in the light of such love as we have in our own hearts. We know how small, how constricted our hearts are, and we are tempted again and again to suppose that God's heart is like our own. Here then is one thing which we must pursue, the knowledge of Jesus as our Lord. Oh, if only we could keep that in the front of our minds, right at the very top of our hearts, how much sweeter and finer life would be. We would be free from many of life's worries and cares because we would always have that steady, sturdy, unfailing assurance: don't you be afraid; you have a Friend, Jesus, your Savior.

GROWTH IN PRAYER

Paul, who grew in his knowledge and understanding of Jesus and the love of God as revealed in the Christ, grew also in the matter of prayer. He no doubt had learned to pray from childhood on, but it was not until he could confidently speak to God as his Father, in the name of Jesus Christ, that prayer took on the prominence in his life which it possessed. No one can read the letters of Paul without being impressed with the presence of prayer in the thought life and missionary career of this great servant of Jesus Christ. He prayed. He prayed for himself. He prayed for his fellow Jews. He prayed for the churches which he founded. He prayed. Prayer was constantly in his heart and on his lips. This is a second area in our spiritual life in which we all have reason to grow. Only the other day a rather successful businessman who holds an important executive position with one of the large businesses in the loop told me what wonderful blessings had come to him through prayer. Oh, so many times, individuals tell me of the almost miraculous answers which God has given them to their simple prayers. God invites us so urgently to pray, and yet what use do you and I make of that privilege? I think it would be a rather sad recital, if we called on each one present this morning and said, "You tell us about your prayer life." I am afraid so many of us would have to say, "My prayers are very intermittent. My prayers are very cold. Usually I pray only when I find myself in trouble." And yet, here God has opened up the well-springs of His mercy. He invites us to ask and assures us that He will give. When Paul said, "I follow after," he meant that he was trying to learn how to pray more as God would have him pray.

GROWTH IN LOVE

Paul also meant that he was trying to grow in love. There was a time when there was not too much love in Paul's heart. He had religion. If you had asked any of his friends or acquaintances, they would have said, Paul was a very religious man, but it was not God's kind of religion. It had no love in it. It was hard and cold. Paul could stand by and hold the garments of the people who killed the first Christian martyr with stones. Paul could persecute the Christians. He could find joy in having them thrown into jail or in the thought that their blood might be shed. He wanted Christianity to be stamped out as a hated thing. That was the state of his heart at that time. There wasn't very much love wasted by Paul on his fellowmen then. And this was the man, who by the power of God's Holy Spirit could come from such a state of heart and mind to that lofty eminence from which he could give expression to the Psalm of Love as we have it in I Corinthians 13 which as you will recall ends with these words, "And now there abide faith, hope, and love, and the greatest of these is love."

"I follow after," said Paul. He never was satisfied with what he had achieved. Even so you and I dare not be satisfied with our achievement as of this day. I am sure that you who are coming to kneel at God's altar this morning have love in your hearts. I have the same confidence that all of you assembled in God's house this morning would like to love. Yet I need not tell you that love flees so quickly and that self-interest, envy, jealousy, bitterness, spite, and hatred readily take their place within our hearts. So here is an area of Christian life in which we must follow after.

GROWTH IN MISSIONARY ZEAL

When Paul said, "I follow after," he also meant that he was trying to share with his fellowmen the things that God had given to him. This was quite exceptional in the Christian life of Paul that he immediately upon his conversion determined to give himself to the task of a Christian minister. He was resolved to tell others what he had found. He had suffered so long under the Law, and he now was so relieved, so happy to have found real peace with God that he wanted all the world to know about that peace. That is why he worked as he worked. He said, he was ready to die, to be damned, if, by so doing, he could save his people. He said he tried to be all things to all men that he might by all means save some. Such was the burning desire in the heart of this man to tell others the story of Jesus Christ.

My friends, do you see why it is important that we must grow, that we must catch the spirit of the apostle who said, "Not as though I had already attained, either were already perfect, but I follow after." He was doing so much, one would imagine that he might have been satisfied. But how can a man be satisfied when he has the story of Jesus to tell to his fellowmen? There can never come a point at which we can be satisfied. And yet how anxious have we been to tell that story? Here we have a fine audience of Christian people. How much anxiety is there in your heart to tell the story of Jesus to other people? This is an area of life in which we must grow. We cannot take for granted that we have achieved. No, we are still so content merely to have the Gospel for ourselves, and what may happen to other people does not worry us very much. This is the best evidence in the world that the real meaning of the Gospel of Jesus Christ has not actually seized us. How can anybody withhold from his fellowmen the story of redemption, if he actually believes it and if this is to him the greatest story ever told? Imagine someone discovering a cure for cancer and then concealing his discovery so that his fellowmen could have no knowledge of it. Could anything be more loveless or more cruel? And yet, here we are, the professing disciples of Jesus Christ who have stood before the cross, whose eyes have been opened by the Spirit of God so that we know, this is the Savior who has taken the sins from the souls of men. When Paul thought of that he said, "Not as though I had already attained, but I must follow after that I might learn how to reach more people."

And so this morning when these younger and these more mature Christians are going to dedicate themselves and their lives to Christ, this is a good time for all of us to vow in our hearts as the Spirit of God gives us strength and understanding that we will not be satisfied with our spiritual attainments, but that we will follow after.

May God to that end be with us and particularly with those who are to be newly received, for Jesus' sake. Amen.

THOUGHTS ON THE HOLY SUPPER

"For I have received of the Lord that which also I delivered unto you. That the Lord Jesus the same night in which He was betrayed took bread: And when He had given thanks, He brake it, and said, Take, eat: this is My body, which is broken for you: this do in remembrance of Me. After the same manner also He took the cup, when He had supped, saying, This cup is the new testament in My blood: this do ye, as oft as ye drink it, in remembrance of Me. For as often as ye eat this bread, and drink this cup, ye do shew the Lord's death till He come. Wherefore whosoever shall eat this bread, and drink this cup of the Lord, unworthily, shall be guilty of the body and blood of the Lord. But let a man examine himself, and so let him eat of that bread, and drink of that cup. For he that eateth and drinketh unworthily, eateth and drinketh damnation to himself, not discerning the Lord's body."—I Corinthians 11: 23-29.

1 1 1

THIS night, my friends, is sacred in the memory of God's children. The occasion which brings us together here this evening really reaches back in time, would we return to its very origins, to a date about 3,500 years ago. The Children of Israel then were held as slaves by the Egyptian people. The time was come when God wanted them liberated and led by Moses into the Land of Promise. Pharaoh, the Egyptian king, refused to accede to the will of God. The Almighty, therefore, found it necessary to lay a heavy hand upon the Egyptian people. He allowed the angel of death to pass over Egypt and to slay the first born both of men and of cattle. Pharaoh, touched by the sorrow of his people, at long last gave the opportunity for Israel's departure. The Children of Israel from that day forth continued annually to commemorate that night.

It was on the night when Jesus and His disciples, together with all the Children of Israel, were observing the Passover Festival, the very night in which He was to be betrayed and to be given over into the hands of His ene-

mies, that He took the opportunity to institute the Holy
Supper. Our texts offers some thoughts on the meaning
and the purpose of this Supper. As the Spirit of God
gives us light and understanding, we want to reflect on
these truths.

WHAT IS THE HOLY SUPPER?

We learn, when we look at these words, first of all,
what the Holy Supper is. We are told, Jesus spoke a
prayer of thanksgiving, took bread, broke it, and said,
" 'Take eat. This is my body which is broken for you.'
. . . After the same manner also He took the cup, when
He had supped, saying, 'This cup is the new testament
in my blood.' " This language seems to be altogether
clear, and yet there has been a great deal of controversy
in the church of Christ about the meaning of Holy Communion. It is as though children engaged in controversy
with one another about the inheritance which was left
them by their parents. Just so God's children have con-
tended and disputed with one another as to the meaning
of Holy Communion. Some have said, "Jesus could not
have meant what His words actually express." They
have insisted that there is no such thing as the real
presence of our Lord's body and blood, but that bread
and wine are merely symbols to their eyes. This view
has been advanced with great vigor. Then there have
been those who have said, "Holy Communion is only a
heavenly gift with nothing of the material and temporal
in it." They have asserted that when the prayer of
thanksgiving is spoken by the ministering servant of
God and the material elements of bread and wine are
consecrated to the use of the Sacrament, that then bread
and wine are changed by a miracle of God into the body
and blood of Jesus. They have eliminated the presence
of the bread and of the wine. The Word of God provides support for neither of those views, howsoever in-

teresting they may sound, and howsoever much they may recommend themselves to human reason. The text stands clear. If you and I want to know what, according to the Word of God, is given to us in Holy Communion, we can learn it very quickly from these words and from other parts of the Sacred Record where the same truth is repeated in almost the identical terminology.

Our text says, "Jesus took bread, gave thanks, and gave it to them saying, 'Take eat, this is my body.'" That makes it simple, not simple to understand, but simple to learn and to believe. When Jesus instituted Holy Communion He gave to His disciples the natural element of bread, but in so doing He gave them by His promise in a super-natural way the body which was to be broken for them. And in like manner He gave them in a natural way the cup, and by His promise in a super-natural way the precious blood which He was going to shed for the redemption of their souls. There are many things in life which you and I do not understand. We do not deny their reality because we do not understand them. Just so we have many things in the Christian faith which we do not understand and which even such Christians accept who have tried to fathom the mystery which lies in Holy Communion. So we accept with simple faith and complete humility what God tells us about the Holy Supper. We believe with our whole hearts that when we receive the bread, Jesus, by His promise and His miracle-working power, in His divine love gives us His body, and with the cup His blood.

THE HOLY SUPPER PROCLAIMS CHRIST'S SACRIFICIAL DEATH

This is one of the wonderful gifts of divine love, and like all other gifts it is intended to serve a beautiful purpose. When Jesus gave Holy Communion to His disciples for the first time He said, "This do in remembrance of Me. This do ye as oft as ye drink it in remembrance of me, for as often as ye eat this bread and drink this cup ye do show the Lord's death till He come." One of the purposes for which our Lord has given us this Holy Supper is this that we, and all those who are His believing disciples, should to the end of time proclaim to the whole human family the story of His sacrificial death.

This is the distinctive characteristic of Christianity. All religions tell men to be good, but only one religion tells us of that One who alone truly was good and who could give Himself as an atoning sacrifice for the sins of all men. It was very interesting to read in a well-known journal that Dr. Toynbee of Oxford, who seems by common consent to be the most noted interpreter of history in our day, said that the world has had only one Savior like Jesus. This man did not approach the subject from the viewpoint of the theologian or from the viewpoint of the Christian, but rather from the viewpoint of the historian. Still, as a historian he had to admit that there is only one Jesus, one who saved as Jesus saved. And this is the task of the Christians by the preaching of the Gospel and by the administration of the Holy Sacrament to proclaim to the end of time the great and blessed truth that Jesus gave Himself for the redemption of the whole human family.

This is God's own interesting, impressive, and dramatic way in which to tell that story. We can afford no hope and bring no real truth and comfort to any human heart except as we can convey to that heart this fact: Jesus died for you. The individual who believes this has found peace, and the individual who does not believe it cannot find peace.

THE HOLY SUPPER A PERSONAL ASSURANCE

But our Lord wanted the Holy Sacrament not merely to be a proclamation of the fact that Jesus had died to save mankind, He wanted it specifically also to be an assurance to each individual.   Jesus, you should understand, did not only die for humanity en masse, but He died for you as an individual.   This makes your appearance at God's altar such a glorious experience for those among you who are communing tonight for the first time.   When you were baptized, Jesus came to you, God the Father came to you, God the Holy Spirit came to you, called you by name, and gave you the assurance of His love for you.   Tonight when you kneel at this altar as the guests of Jesus it is as though the Saviour came to each one of you and said, "Take my body. I gave it for *you*. Receive this cup, my own precious blood. I shed it for *you*."   There lies the power and the benefit of this wonderful gift.   There we once again have such an eloquent expression of the love which is in the heart of God for each one of us.

We so often forget that.   When we encounter difficulties in life, when sorrow and heartaches overtake us, we are all inclined to forget that God loves us.   He never wants us to forget, however.   He always wants it to be right in the front of our minds, very vividly and clearly before the eye of faith so that whatever the circumstances of life may be, we never lose sight of this truth, *my Lord loves me*.   Oh, that is what He wants to impress on you tonight.   That is what He wants to write into the heart of each one of you indelibly so that it should be right there in life and in death, in good days and in bad, in moments of delirious joy and extreme pleasure and in those moments when all seems dark and hopeless. Always, always, there should shine that one light, "My Lord loves me.   When I knelt at that altar, He said to me, 'This is my body given for you, and this is my blood shed for you.' "

You see how circumspectly Jesus has made provision for us, how He has tried to follow us, to put His arms of love around us, so that we will not get lost or be overtaken by sin and evil and drawn away from Him. He wants to stay close to us. His love should be the one dominant truth in all our lives. I hope that each of you, receiving this blessed gift, will carry that gracious blessing of divine love away with you in your hearts to your homes, to your several tasks.

HOW TO RECEIVE THE HOLY SUPPER

Well, if you are to receive Holy Communion with such blessing, then you must come with a heart properly prepared. The Christians at Corinth had not been doing so well in this matter and Paul had to speak to them very frankly. When they came together for the celebration of Holy Communion, they misused it. They acted as though they were getting together for a banquet. They were overlooking the spiritual significance of the occasion. So Paul had to warn them. This is what he said: "Wherefore, whosoever shall eat this bread and drink this cup of the Lord unworthily shall be guilty of the body and the blood of the Lord." To prevent this he advised, "Let a man examine himself and so let him eat of that bread and drink of that cup, for he that eateth and drinketh unworthily eateth and drinketh damnation to himself, not discerning the Lord's body." He told these Christians at Corinth, "If you are going to get together and celebrate Holy Communion as though it were just another meal, then you will not receive forgiveness for your sins. You will rather be adding sins to the sins you already have, because you will be abusing the body and the blood of Jesus. Beware of that, and, lest you come in an unworthy way, examine yourselves." This Holy Supper was given for sinners, so they should look into their hearts and see whether they thought that they were sinners.

This counsel still holds. Holy Communion is only for sinners. No one who is not a sinner can receive Holy Communion with blessing and with benefit because in Holy Communion Jesus said, "This is my body which I gave for you." Why should He give His body for someone who is not a sinner? So look into your heart. Be honest with God and with yourself. If you will look into your heart, you will have no trouble discovering sin. It is only the person who closes his eyes, and who refuses to look at his own state of soul who can be self-satisfied. If you compare your life with what God asks of you, then it should be very easy for you to hang your head in shame and penitence as before your heavenly Father who is so good to you.

But it is not enough to know that you are a sinner. If you wish to receive Holy Communion with blessing, then you must come as a sinner who is not only penitent but who also desires the mercy and the forgiveness of God. Some folks know that they are sinners, but they are not in the least bit sorry for their sins. Sometimes you hear individuals boastfully tell how drunk they got on a given occasion. Sometimes you hear men boast how clever they were in cheating somebody else in a business deal of one kind or another. Sometimes you hear people boast about the sins of uncleanness in which they live. Sometimes you hear people boast about their demonic temper and biting, cutting, killing tongue. So you see, not everybody who knows that he is a sinner is ashamed of his sins and anxious to have them forgiven. But everyone who wants to be a grateful and richly blessed guest at the Lord's table must come not only with a consciousness of guilt, but also with the feeling of sorrow for sin and with the desire to have that sin taken away, completely forgiven.

But even that is not enough. Jesus did not only say that the Holy Supper was for sinners. He said that here was the body which He gave and the blood which He shed for the forgiveness of sins. I have known individuals who wanted to go to the Holy Supper not because they wanted Jesus to give them something, but because they really thought they were going to do something for Jesus. They were going to prove to God how good they were by coming to Holy Communion, and thus they were going to earn their own forgiveness. I have on occasion had to say to someone, "Holy Communion is for helpless sinners. Since you claim to be able to work out your own salvation, Holy Communion is not for you." Look into your hearts. See if you believe that Jesus gave Himself for you and that He is now going to give you His assurance of love under the seal of the blessed Sacrament. If you believe this, then come with glad hearts.

This word 'worthily' or 'unworthily' disturbs a lot of people. They have a wrong conception of it. They think that only those people who are really good can go to Holy Communion. Sometimes such people say to me, "I would like to go to Holy Communion, but I do not think I have been good enough." They mean to say that they are conscious of sin and that they must live a better life before they can go to the Lord's table. My friends, don't wait for that. If you know that you are a sinner; if you want God's forgiveness; and if you believe that Jesus has earned it for you, then come, because Holy Communion is for you.

You can understand from what has been said, I think, why we practice with reference to the administration of the Lord's Supper as we do. Sometimes folks think we are not as generous as we ought to be in the administration of the Holy Supper. They feel we ought to extend an invitation to everyone and anyone who may be in the Lord's house when the Holy Supper is being

administered to come forward to the Lord's table. They
think it should not be denied any sinner. This in a sense
is true, but as you can see from these words of our text,
the sinner must understand what Holy Communion is
before he can receive it with benefit. That is why we
insist upon a number of things. First of all, we insist
that individuals who are going to receive Holy Communion should have been instructed so that they know
what the Holy Supper is, what it is that Jesus instituted,
and why. We insist that they should know how to examine
themselves, for after all, God has made the church the
steward of His mysteries. He has a right, and people
have a right, to expect that the church will be faithful
in the fulfillment of its stewardship responsibilities. So
if it is for us to be the guardians of this Holy Sacrament
and to be the guardians of men's immortal souls, as God
gives these souls into our care, we should try, as faith-
fully as we can, under God, to fulfill that responsibility.
If we have any in our audience this evening who are
not affiliated with us, we certainly do not want them to
think that we conceive of ourselves as the holy people,
who are good enough to receive Holy Communion, and
of them as people who are not good enough. No, it is a
question of knowing, of being able to examine yourself,
and of having a faith with which alone anyone can receive the Lord's Supper as a blessing to his soul.

This explains also why we provide opportunity for
those who wish to be guests at the Lord's Table to sig-
nify their intention to the pastor beforehand. This gives
us the opportunity of dealing with individual souls and
of explaining to them whatever may require explanation.
We are not trying to withhold the Holy Sacrament from
anyone. We are rather eager that it should be received
by the largest possible number of people. If we have
any in our audience this evening who desire to have the

privilege of being blessed guests at the Lord's Table, we certainly would be ready to spend whatever time it might require to impart to them the instructions as given in God's own Holy Book so that all such might rejoice with us in the use of this divine gift of heavenly love.

May it please God to be with you, each of you, who will come forward, and to allow you to receive with blessing for time and for eternity what Jesus has made possible for you by His death on the cross and by His institution of the Holy Supper.

THE DYING CHRIST

"When Jesus therefore had received the vinegar, He said, 'It is finished:' and He bowed His head, and gave up the ghost."—John 19: 30.

1   1   1

A GREAT host of God's children are about the foot of our Savior's cross this day. They are looking up into the face of The Dying Christ. John in his Holy Gospel, the nineteenth chapter, the thirtieth verse says, "He bowed His head and gave up the ghost."

MOMENTS OF JOY

This was the end, the end of the most beautiful life ever lived here on earth, a life in which there had been moments of sweet joy and happiness. We can be sure that our blessed Lord was made happy by the love of His mother, by the affectionate care of His foster father. He enjoyed the gifts of the Father on high as He saw them in the hills and the valleys, in the grass and the flowers. He loved to speak of these things. We know that it brought happiness to Him when He could take little ones upon His knee and bless them. It was always an occasion of joy for Him when young and old, rich and poor gathered about Him so that He could break unto them the Bread of Life. There were moments of exquisite happiness when He could feed the hungry and heal the sick. His heart was filled with gladness when the poor, humble woman came to Him, bathed His feet with tears of repentance and dried them with her tresses. Joy filled His soul when a Roman Centurion or a Syrophenician woman gave expression to a strong, firm faith. These were the moments of happiness in the ministry of our Lord.

SIN BRINGS SORROW AND DEATH

But while He had these moments, the overtones of sorrow and of sadness also were ever present. It was not a matter of joy to be born in a barn or to be compelled to flee from the sword of a treacherous, murderous King Herod. Our Lord's ministry began in a very severe way. He spent forty days and forty nights wrestling with God in prayer and battling against the Tempter. His most intimate disciples often disappointed Him. It was not long before the enemies began to plot against Him. They hated Him with an unrelenting hatred. They wanted to be rid of Him. They were not satisfied until after all His heartache, suffering, and sadness they nailed Him to a cross. And there "He bowed His head and gave up the ghost." That was the end.

That, my friends, is always the end when you are dealing with the consequences of sin. As we look up into the face of our blessed Lord and see Him, the dying Savior on the cross, we cannot but be terrified by the fact that our Lord has given up the ghost, for it teaches us what the consequences of sin really are. Sin always kills. It doesn't make any difference where you find it, or in what shape or form, or in what circumstance. Sin always kills whatever it touches. Little children are playing with their toys. They are having a lot of fun. Then one of them becomes selfish and wants all the toys for himself. At once, laughter and playing cease as strife and discord enter in. Joy has been killed.—The family is happily gathered and all is going well. There is peace in the household. Then one member in the family becomes self-willed, stubborn, disobedient. The family peace is gone. Sin has killed it. Sin always kills. God gives wonderful gifts to the individual, endows him richly. His life has every promise. But then he gives way to sin. Sin enslaves him more and more. Before he knows it, his manhood is killed. His powers have been destroyed. He is but a caricature of what he might have been. Sin always kills. God pours out His bounties over a land so rich as ours. There is an abundance for all. But there are those who do not wish to share, those who would have all they can grasp for themselves no matter by what means, whether fair or foul, just so they get what they want. Then strife and conflict enter in. Men lie at each other's throats. Once again, sin kills.

But worst of all, sin takes men away from God. It builds walls between them and their Creator. It separates them from the Author of life. They find themselves in darkness. They are cast out. They are forever dead. Sin kills.

JESUS DIED TO OVERCOME DEATH

But Jesus came into this world to do away with sin. So He had to die. He could not stop until He had been nailed to the appointed cross, bowed His head and given up the ghost, for the whole terrible tragedy of sin had to work itself out in Him. He hung there as the substitute of the whole human family. So as you and I look up this night into the face of the Dying Christ and we see Him bow His head and give up the ghost, we can only come before our Creator with shame and sorrow in our hearts. Our heads bowed, we must acknowledge that we are the fault of this. It is we and our sins who have nailed Him to the cross and brought Him to His death.

As we look up into the face of this Dying Christ, we also find hope. If what we have done to Christ terrifies us and fills us with shame and remorse, then what He brings us provides us with hope and peace. For this is the Christ who took away the sins of the world. This is He who bore our sins in His own body on the tree that we might be redeemed and reconciled. We see here the Lamb of God for sinners slain to make complete atonement for all of our transgressions. If you came here with a sense of uneasiness, if you are troubled by an inner spirit of restlessness, if you do not have quite that feeling of peace and inner calm which you desire, if your conscience is saying unto you, "All is not well," if you are worried and troubled about what tomorrow may bring, because you are not sure of God's love and His protecting care, then look once again into the face of this Dying Christ. See Him for what He is, the One who was wounded for your transgressions and bruised for your iniquities, so that you might have peace with God.

Remember, it doesn't make any difference what your sins may be, "Though they be as scarlet, yet they shall be made white as snow." "Where sin hath become mighty the grace of God hath become yet mightier." There is no sin in the long list of human wrongdoing for which there is no forgiveness in and through this Christ. The only way you can lose it is by rejecting Him. There is only one sin which condemns, the sin against the Holy Spirit, that is, the refusal to accept the truth of salvation of which He would persuade you. If you are ready to let the Spirit of God give you strength to embrace this Christ and say, "My Lord, who has redeemed me, a lost and condemned sinner," then you should be sure, that God, as He looks down upon you, sees not your sins but the holiness of Christ which covers all of your transgressions.

CHRIST'S DEATH ATTESTS HIS LOVE

My friends, this wonderful fact that Jesus gave Himself for us should give us the further assurance that in Him we have a Friend who loves us. As you look up into the face of the Dying Christ on the cross, you should realize that "greater love than this hath no man, than that he lay down his life for his brethren." The apostle argued this way. He said, "If God spared not His only-begotten Son, how then should He not also with Him freely give us every good thing?" We have many needs of body, of mind, and of soul, but we do not have a single need in which Jesus is not ready to help us, to befriend us, to care for us, to provide for us.

So search the corners of your mind and of your heart. What is worrying you tonight? Are you worried about your business and about the uncertainties of tomorrow? Are you worried about your job; or about the fact that your pay check does not quite reach to make ends meet as prices rise; or what is it you are worrying about tonight? Are you probably troubled because you are looking forward to an operation; or hasn't your heart been behaving itself so well; or are your nerves raw and tense and jangled; or do you have some problem in your home with which you do not know quite how to cope? Is one of your children giving you a great deal of heartache and sorrow? What are you worrying about tonight? Whatever it may be, look up into the face of that Christ, that Dying Christ, and see His infinite love. It embraces your every want. Talk to Him about your cares. Take Him into your confidence. Let Him be your Ally, your Friend, your Counsellor, and your Guide. Remember, He is right at your bedside while you are sleeping. He is with you while you are working. He rides with you as you go to work and come home again. He is always with you. "Lo, I am with you always," He said.

But as you drink in this love and have one more look into the face of this Dying Christ, as you begin to realize how much He has loved you, you feel that you must love Him, too. Because He hath first loved us, that is why we want to love Him. Perhaps you have not been too conscious of this. Maybe Jesus has not played a very important part in your life. Probably you have been so busy with other things. Perhaps your heart and mind have been so engrossed with the things of this life and of this world that you have not had very much time for your best Friend. Well, form the resolution now, in this sacred hour, that as the Spirit of God gives you strength, light, and understanding, you will love your Savior, love His Word, love His Holy Sacraments, love the privilege of speaking with Him in prayer, love to do His holy work. In that direction lies nobility of soul, loveliness of spirit and of character, beauty of life. In that direction lies true, deep, satisfying joy and happiness. Sin kills, but the Spirit of God, who works faith and who ignites the fires of love within our hearts, He brings life and hope, peace and joy.

May God in His infinite mercy inscribe indelibly upon the heart of each of us the image of the Dying Christ and give to each of us that faith, that hope, that love which can come only through Him.

A FACT AND A PROMISE

"Knowing that He which raised up the Lord Jesus shall raise up us also by Jesus, and shall present us with you."—II Corinthians 4:14.

GOOD FRIDAY ended on a note of tragedy. We heard, "He bowed His head and gave up the ghost." That, so far as man knew, was the end. Death in the experience of mankind had always been a one way, dead end street. Even the Greeks, universally renowned to this day because of their philosophical insight and their scientific understanding, had never managed to find an answer to death. Death ended it all. That is why their great dramas, portraying the experiences of mankind, always ended on a note of tragedy and hopelessness. It was not until Jesus came that this situation was changed. But with Jesus we get a new note.

JESUS AROSE

His enemies had not expected it. But Jesus surprised the enemies. This is how our text tells it, II Corinthians 4:14. We read, "He which raised up the Lord Jesus shall raise up us also by Jesus." You will notice we have here both a fact and a promise. The fact: He raised up the Lord Jesus.

This is a very remarkable fact, remarkable from various points of view. First of all, this fact had been foretold. God had promised that a Savior was going to come long before Jesus was born. He had told where and when He was to be born and under what circumstances. He had told that He was to be a Savior who would suffer and die, but, unbelievable as it would seem to us today, He also told that He was going to rise again. The holy writer addressing himself to God said by divine inspiration, "Thou wilt not suffer thine Holy One to see corruption." He was speaking of the Mes-

siah.   Others who had died should turn to dust and
ashes, but not the Messiah.   He should not see corruption.

Our Lord's enemies did not plan it that way.   They
were satisfied when they succeeded in nailing Jesus to
the cross.   They believed that even as death had always
ended things for man so death would also end the career
of Jesus Christ.   Once they had Him on the cross, once
He had bowed His head and given up the ghost, they
really did not need to be very much worried about Him
any more.   They knew that not only the prophets of the
Old Testament, but Jesus too, had spoken of His resurrection.   He had said, "Destroy this temple and in three
days I will raise it up again."   He had assured His disciples, He must die, but He would rise and go before
them in Galilee to company with them, to give them such
further instructions, directions, and guidance as they
required.   The opponents of Jesus knew of this promise,
but they did not believe it.   They feared, however, that
the disciples might perpetrate a fraud.   They might steal
our Lord's body from the tomb and spread the legend
that He had risen.   So they tried to guard against such
trickery.   The tomb was sealed.   A Roman military
guard was placed about it.   No man, they were sure,
would do violence to a Roman military guard.   Now they
felt certain that Jesus was dead and gone.   But it was
not so to be.   When God's hour was come, He raised
Him up.

This, my friends, is a fact most firmly established.
Not only was it foretold, but it was a fact which the
disciples knew to be true and of which they were so completely persuaded as to be ready to die rather than to
deny it.   The angels of God said it was so.   When Peter,
James, and John came rushing to the tomb on that first
Easter Sunday they encountered heavenly messengers

who said, "Why seek ye the living among the dead? He is not here. He is risen." Jesus proclaimed His victory over death. He appeared to His disciples. He spoke with them. He gave them repeated opportunities to know that He lived. God raised Him up from the dead. This was so clear and so sure to the early disciples that no truth played a more prominent part in early Christianity. A number of writers in modern times who have undertaken to write about Jesus have quite correctly emphasized this particular point. "He lives." That was the *one* dynamic, driving fact in the lives of the early Christians.

A PROMISE

My friends, this truth that He lives is not merely an isolated historical event, howsoever wonderful and glorious it may have been, but still only an event which is of no particular meaning or consequence for us. No, this is an event which is most intimately related to us, to our own interests, to our own hopes. Our text gives us not only the fact but *along with the fact a promise.* "He which raised up the Lord Jesus *shall raise us up also by Jesus.*"

This fact that God raised up Jesus has meaning for us. It gives to us an assurance that our God loves us. When little children do things they ought not to do their consciences bother them. They feel ashamed of themselves. They get to be on the defensive. Sometimes they become ugly and mean. Well, we are the little children of our heavenly Father. The things we do that we ought not to do are the most disturbing factors in our lives. They are the things that make us feel ashamed. It is because of these we should like to hide away from God. It is because of these there is fear in our hearts. We do not know what will happen in a world which is governed by a God whom we have offended and whose

Holy Will we have transgressed. And now comes the message of Easter. It assures us that the God who raised up Jesus loves us and is ready to raise us up also. Jesus has taken our sins away. The very fact that the Father hath raised Him up should be to us an assurance that even as He was delivered for our offenses so was He raised for our justification. Our sins have been atoned for. All fear should be gone. Joy and peace should fill our souls.

But this very love which God now has toward us should call forth a corresponding love from within our own hearts. If it be true, as it is, that the God who raised up Jesus is going to raise us up, that all our sins have been taken away and that our heavenly Father looks down upon us with pleasure as upon His dearly beloved children, then we cannot but respond with love. You will remember Jesus put it this way. When a poor sinner who had sinned grievously was so grateful because all sins were forgiven He explained, "This sinner is so grateful because she has received so much love and so much forgiveness."

That is the way it must be with us as we become more and more conscious of the love which God has for us. There must flow from our hearts a love toward Him, a love which expresses itself in our relationship to our fellowmen. If you become conscious of the fact that God loves you, that He has taken all your sins away through Christ, then you will strive to express that love. You will try to show it in your own home in relationship to your dear ones. You will try by the very love which you have toward your spouse, toward your children, toward your parents, your brothers and sisters to contribute to the spirit of happiness and peace within your family life.

Here in this love which comes to us from God who is going to raise us up as He raised Jesus up, we have also the power which makes it possible for us to contribute to a finer happiness and to a more peaceful and satisfying relationship among men at large. You and I stand in various relationships as citizens, as working people, as business people, as members of the human family. Here in the love which God shows us He points for us the direction in which we should go, if we want to resolve the great social problems of our time and create a greater measure of happiness and finer relationships among men.

Here, too, lies our hope. He who raised up Jesus will raise up us also. Just think how sad and tragic it would be, if life were only the drab and uninteresting thing we often find it to be. Imagine the poor wife and mother who yields up her energies in the bearing of her children, in the performance of her daily tasks day after day and week upon week. She is imprisoned in her little kitchen working from early morn until late at night, wearing herself out in endless labors. Or think of the man who gets up, puts on his overalls and probably with his lunch basket in his hand trudges off day after day to the same job, to do the same little stint for the same small reward. And after he has worked for years and years and years, what has he got? Perhaps he has no money in the bank. Perhaps he is glad, if he has been able to pay the rent and buy the food and keep the children clothed. Is that what life means? Do we just go on slaving, the meanwhile going down and down and down to death? Has there ever been a time in your life when you have said to yourself, what is this all about? Is this worth the candle? Why keep on struggling like this?

Well, thoughts like that came even to the apostle Paul. Paul said, "If we Christians have hope only in

this life then we are the most miserable of all people."
Here we are trying to crucify the flesh with all its evil
lusts. Here we are, trying to deny ourselves the carnal
delights for which the evil heart longs and hungers. We
are trying to live a life that will be pleasing unto God
and then of a sudden the whole show is over, the curtain
falls, and what have we had? If we have no hope, we
have not had very much.

Even the people who try to get something out of this
life don't have very much. Within very recent weeks
I sat with a man who was worth more than half a million dollars in cold cash. As we discussed his life and
his needs of soul, he said, "I have an abundance of
money, but I have no love and I have no happiness." I
think of the poor woman who said not too long ago, "Oh,
I cannot complain about money. My husband gives me
all the money I want. He buys me anything I desire, but
that is not what I want. What I want is love, happiness." You see, if we have only the things of this life,
or, if as Christians, we deny ourselves many of those
fleshly, carnal things, then what have we? What is the
use of living? We can then understand the old Romans
who opened their veins and bled to death.

My friends, let us look at it another way. Imagine
that here you have a surgeon and there you have a
patient. If the surgeon in looking at the patient sees
only an ugly wound, and flowing blood, and an offensive
infection to be drained, if he sees only broken and
crushed bone, then why should he bother? But that is
not what the surgeon sees. The surgeon sees all of that,
but he looks beyond that. He sees that patient restored,
restored to health, strength, to the full renewed vigor
of manhood or womanhood, as the case might be. And
so he goes to work. Thus it is with us. If we have
nothing but sweat, suffering, tears and death to expect,

then why live. But that is not the promise. The promise reads, "He which raised up the Lord Jesus shall raise up us also by Jesus." When we have that promise then we can look forward. Then we know that there lies ahead a glorious heritage. We can face whatever the problems and difficulties of life may be for we know that beyond this time there is a heavenly heritage which shall afford us fullness of joy and pleasures forevermore.

And, my friends, this wonderful hope which brings ever again renewed courage and strength into our lives also serves to dry our tears and to heal our wounds of heart, when we have been saddened by the loss of a dear one. A Christian may feel very keenly the loss of one who was near and dear, but when he thinks of the fulfillment of this promise given to us in or text, then he can smile even through his tears, and out of the depths of his heart sing the praises of God. He knows that the dear one has gone to be with God. It is as the fine Christian lady said to me recently, "I thank God that my husband is relieved. Now I know he doesn't have to suffer anymore."

May it please the Spirit of God in His infinite grace and mercy to impress upon our hearts and our minds clearly and unforgettably this great fact: "God raised up Jesus Christ," and this beautiful promise: "He which raised up the Lord Jesus shall raise up us also by Jesus."